SAVE A LIFE TAKE A LIFE

GREEN BERET MEDIC IN VIETNAM AND THE PASSAGE HOME

PETER MCSHANE

Lost Parachute Press LLC
New York

Save a Life–Take a Life, Green Beret Medic in Vietnam & The Passage Home

For information about this title or to order additional books and/or electronic media, contact the publisher:

Lost Parachute Press LLC
202 Churchill Lane
Fayetteville, NY 13066

These stories are a work of creative nonfiction and represents the author's recollections and those of other Special Forces operatives, together with after-action reports and miscellaneous reference material. The names of the characters have been changed to protect their identity.

Author's website: *http://www.petermcshane.com*

The following chapters were originally published (some in slightly different form) in the following publications:
"Prologue" (Why I Write) *New York Times Warrior Voices/interactive, 2013*
"Minefield" in *Syracuse Intertext Magazine, 2013*
"VA Shrink" in *O-Dark-Thirty, 2014*
"Perez" in *Sunday Stories-Vol. 1 Brooklyn, 2015*
"Little Pine Creek Club" in *Shooter Literary Magazine, 2015*
"Daddy, Did You Kill Anybody in Vietnam?" in *The Weight of My Armor, 2016*
"Al" in *Proud To Be: Writing by American Warriors, Vol. 4, 2015*

ISBNs: 978-1-7322654-0-0 (print)
978-1-7322654-1-7 (eBook)

Printed in the United States of America.

First Edition: May 2018

10 9 8 7 6 5 4 3 2 1

For my brothers in arms

De Oppresso Liber

Table of Contents

Prologue

I wrote this story because I wanted to know why. I became a moneychanger with the empty suits and charlatans, the social and economic elite, the pinky rings and silver spoons; we had nothing in common. They never served. Their sons and daughters never served. They went to the Country Club, flew to Monaco and St. Moritz, managed their investments, traveled to homes in the mountains and on the seacoast. They'd court customers in good times and kick them out when times were tough. I held them in contempt for turning their backs and was fired for insubordination. If not for my VA pension, I'd be traveling from park bench to cardboard box. I want to know why; why didn't I play the game?

When I left the service, I put my military memorabilia in a box and stored it away, out of sight. I wanted no part of that memory to cloud my future. I would see the box every time we moved and try to leave it behind, but the box followed me everywhere, and the memories caught up with me. They came to me in nightmares; they came to me while I dined with my wife; they came to me while I drove in the passing lane on the interstate; they came to me while I walked in the forest. I wanted to know why; why I felt remorse, fear, anger.

I wanted to know why the captain grandstanded and got us shot; why I saved his life, but couldn't save others more worthy; why they napalmed the camp while Tommy was still there; why I chose not to return to my team; why I trusted no one; why I pushed the people away who cared for me; why I compromised my humanity; why we had to pay the price for others' cowardice; why the bullet merely grazed my heart, letting me live. I wanted to know why, so I parried with the memory fragments.

I wrote, and I parried. I wrote, and it hurt. I wrote, and I cried. I wrote, and soon the pain diminished.

PART I

WAR ZONE–AN AWAKENING

Cam Ranh Bay

The Northwest Orient charter left Seattle in a blinding December rain, crammed with GIs for the 24-hour flight to Vietnam, off to fight the politicians' war. We refueled in Japan, long enough to stretch our legs and buy snacks. The stewardesses were not like the ones on flights I've taken since. They were sullen and dressed like pallbearers in white blouses and navy-blue suits. We were a plane full of cherries, 120 days in the service, most of us, but that didn't matter. I was the exception with over a year of Special Forces training, but still we didn't know what to expect. We were full of ourselves; gung ho, brimming with the propaganda they fed us in training. None of us in that plane had tasted real fear. It was all practice up until now.

At the beginning of the journey, I felt like I was on the team bus headed for a high school football game. Most of the soldiers were teenagers. The guy sitting next to me looked like he hadn't started shaving yet. There was a lot of hooting and hollering and talking shit. The boasting went on for a few hours until we settled in for the long flight, and after that the mood cooled. We slept, read, or just stared into space. Other than an occasional laugh, mostly nervous outbursts, the mood was somber. I wondered how many of us would make the return trip.

I looked around at the faces, the blank stares. Were they having second thoughts about the mission? I was. Looking out the window of the jetliner as we approached Vietnam, I was struck by the beauty of the South China Sea and the coastline. It looked like St. Thomas: pure white sand and water a thousand shades of blue and green. I imagined running on the beach, feet toying with the surf, full of the beauty, fragrance, and hope of the day, full of myself.

"This is your Captain speaking. We're ten minutes out of Cam Ranh Bay. The airport experiences frequent mortar attacks and rocket fire, so we're going to employ defensive maneuvers on our approach to the runway. Fasten your seatbelts."

He didn't say how often aircraft were hit. No one talked as the plane circled downward, losing altitude as it slipped through airspace. I looked out the window, the bay below framing the runway on one side and jungle on the other. I could see gun emplacements, sandbag bunkers and tanks, APCs, and deuce-and-a-halfs lining the airstrip. The hair on the back of my neck stiffened like the hackles of a fighting cock. Waiting for the plane to explode in a ball of fire, I sat catatonic in my seat as we continued our descent to the airport. We were floating, the engines silent, the plane wallowing as it fell. Then it shuddered as we touched down, tires screeching on the tarmac.

I heard sighs of relief as I loosened my death grip on the arms of the seat. We taxied to the end of the runway and came to a stop a hundred meters from the nearest building. It didn't look much like an airport: no big, modern terminal; just a hodgepodge of temporary buildings and tents. The view out the window sure looked like a war zone, but to my amazement there was no rifle fire, no mortars, and no rockets. Airport workers walked around the plane with little regard for their safety. Hell, they weren't even armed. They rolled a jetway up to the plane's door, and as it swung open, the first soldiers out stood in the doorway, carefully surveying the situation; there were no enemies in sight. Relieved, we deplaned into waiting buses.

The Cam Ranh Bay Repo Depot was a sprawling military complex of tents and makeshift structures that housed enough administrative personnel to process troops in and out of the country. At any one time, the processing center housed several thousand troops going or coming. We gathered our belongings and prepared to have them inspected. It was the usual hurry-up-and-wait Army program. The lines were long and slow moving. As I approached an inspector, I could see that he was going through all of the baggage. I panicked. I had smuggled a Browning 9mm pistol with a 25-round magazine into country, not wanting to use a WWII-vintage Army issue 45. The Browning was contraband, but I hadn't expected to be shaken down.

The inspector went through the bags in front of mine. I opened my duffel and grabbed the pistol, palmed it, and slipped it between my belt and the small of my back. There was a guy ahead of me and as I pushed the duffel down the long table, the pistol slipped past my belt down into my briefs. I could feel the cold steel against the crack of my ass. It was all I could do to maintain my composure. I waddled, fearful that the pistol would fall to the floor. Several steps further I could see the inspector watching me as I pushed my duffel in front of him.

"Are you okay, soldier? You look like you're in pain."

"Sergeant, my back is killing me after that plane ride."

He stared at me for what seemed minutes. I held my breath, expecting him to call the MPs to pat me down, but instead he grimaced and shook his head.

"Once you get to your barracks, try lying on the floor. Go to sick call tomorrow and ask the medics for a couple of Darvon; that works for me."

I took a deep breath.

"Thanks, Sarge."

He flipped through my belongings and pushed the duffel back to me.

"Hope you feel better, soldier."

Relieved and smiling to myself, I waddled over to the nearest latrine where I retrieved the pistol.

We were issued jungle fatigues and boots and instructed to put anything we didn't want to keep in country into a shipping box for the trip home to the States. I stuffed my dress uniform, shirt, tie, socks, and white underwear into the cardboard box, along with my polished boots, and addressed it to my mother. I pushed the sealed carton full of my personal effects across the table to a soldier who loaded it into a shipping container, then closed the heavy steel door. I wondered whether that stuff would be all the memory she'd have of me.

The base was a sea of soldiers. I could tell the difference between us FNGs and seasoned soldiers, especially the infantry. Deeply tanned, their uniforms well-worn and faded, they looked strung-out on dope, or just plain spent. Some had colorful scarves or hats or jackets, something that individualized their experience, picked up somewhere during their tour. One guy had a thin red silk scarf tied over the crown of his head under his army baseball cap. Another had cut the pant legs off his jungle fatigues, de rigueur in the field, but not in garrison. You couldn't get away with lax dress code stateside, but here, pretty much anything was okay. The brass generally didn't fuck with short-timers, but they would not tolerate trophy VC fingers and ears hanging like jewelry around a soldier's neck.

I spent a week in a holding company waiting for orders to ship out to Nha Trang, the headquarters for Special Forces. My time there was relatively free of the menial duty relegated to low-rank enlisted personnel. I was upset that I hadn't received orders for the promotion to sergeant our class had been promised before shipping out, so I took matters into my own hands and sewed on three stripes. It was easy to rationalize. We were the military's most highly skilled medics. Why would the army spend $100,000 training us only to do KP, police cigarette butts, and paint rocks when we could be doing really important work like saving lives at the MASH?

The sergeant's stripes disappeared before leaving for Nha Trang. I could have landed in the brig if someone had read my orders and realized that I had been impersonating a noncommissioned officer, but I knew I could get away with it. We were trained to take calculated risks.

Nha Trang

We cleared Cam Ranh Bay and headed up Route 1, a two-lane macadam highway that wound through hill country near the coast. The 35-klick ride to Nha Trang in the back of an open deuce-and-a-half with three unarmed GIs was nerve wracking. Only the soldier riding shotgun had an M-16. It was a perfect setup for an ambush. I was hypervigilant, waiting for an AK-47 bullet to the head that would end my tour before it started. I felt like one of those moving targets at the shooting range.

The luxuriant green hills and tilled fields seemed to undulate as the road unfolded, swallowing the truck in shades of greens and browns. The air was pungent with the acrid smell of cooking fires, yet fragrant like a woman's perfume. Bougainvillea engulfed the road, the lush bushes caressing the truck as we passed. Flower gardens with roses, gardenia, jasmine, and scores of other tropical flowers dotted the landscape. The sky was as blue as I had ever seen. Farmers toiled in their fields, some terraced on the side of hills, seeming to defy gravity. Villagers waved at the huge truck as if we were tourists. The scene might have been Shangri La, except every moment I anticipated a grenade landing in the back of the truck, lobbed by an innocent-looking peasant woman working in the fields by the side of the road.

Nha Trang is a seaside port city nestled in the coastal hills, about 450 klicks from Saigon. Its sandy beaches and tropical climate drew vacationers. The Special Forces base, one of several military installations, was surrounded by a chain-link fence with a guard shack that opened onto a city street. Driving through the gate to the compound, I felt the tension in my gut release, like air escaping from a punctured tire.

I'd been assigned to Tactical Zone III, headquartered in Bien Hoa. It would take a few days to cut my orders, so I was stuck in Nha Trang over the Christmas holiday. As a low-ranking enlisted man, I was plenty busy just trying to make myself scarce. If you looked like you needed something to do, you'd wind up on KP or guard duty. It was a lonely time for me. My family always made a big deal over Christmas. The whole clan gathered for Midnight Mass followed by breakfast, a gift exchange, and long talks with Mom, Dad, Alice, and Matt. My brother was in charge of making the holiday punch, a lethal combination of Irish whisky, rum, heavy cream, and eggs. My sister could always be counted on to entertain us with her peculiar choices in dates. I recalled that last year she had introduced us to Sid, who drove up to the house in a late model red Cadillac convertible with a white top. He had white hair, a gut that spilled over his belt, and a red blazer about four sizes too big for his shrunken shoulders. I thought he had to be pushing 70.

I passed the time reading and watching the three movies they had: Cat Ballou, A Fistfull of Dollars, and The Good, The Bad and The Ugly. They played over and over in a Quonset hut they called the Entertainment Hooch. A former motor pool, the word "entertainment" was dramatically inaccurate. The smell of motor oil and grease pervaded the place after the building had baked all day in the tropical sun. Folding chairs were lined up wide and deep on either side of a center aisle. In the back of the building on a steel desk was a 16mm projector. Two speakers were set up in front on either side of a pull-down screen like the one at my high school. I loved the movies, and Clint Eastwood was the man I wanted to be: tough and fearless, with a soft spot. I didn't think that I'd have any room for softness in Nam, at least not from what I'd been told in training. Jane Fonda played a plucky and independent woman and I was in love. Less than two years later she was to become the voice of the antiwar movement, and in 1972 was nicknamed, "Hanoi Jane" for a trip she took to North Vietnam.

On Christmas Eve, I went into the city to have a look around. I was taken aback by its charm and vibrancy. The buildings were a mixture of French villas and Indochinese architecture, interspersed with the sprawl of makeshift vendor stalls. The streets teemed with people, walking, shopping, and relaxing in outdoor cafes. You could buy anything from sidewalk vendors: transistor radios, American cigarettes, Cuban cigars, even popular English-language magazines. To my surprise, most vendors could speak some English, so it wasn't difficult to do business. While they'd always ask to be paid in US dollars rather than the Vietnamese dong, we had strict orders to use only the local currency.

The food tended to be spicy, heavy with chilies or curry. That day, I tried a plate of rice noodles with shrimp sauce, and a spicy bowl of fish soup. Vietnam was my introduction to spicy food and I was hooked. We never had it at home because my father had chronic heartburn. I could see why the Vietnamese were slender. The meals were filling, but not heavy like Western food. In the afternoon, I took a cyclo ride to the edge of the city and into the foothills. An imposing statue of the Buddha at least 100 feet tall stood guard in the hills overlooking the city. Nearby were an ancient pagoda, flower gardens, and a shrine with a statue of a reclining Buddha, as long as the Buddha overlooking the city was tall. Hundreds of people had come to worship. I saw many Westerners that day: Germans, French, and a group of Norwegians on a bus tour. I was flabbergasted to find that a large population of Europeans lived and worked in country, in addition to those who came on holiday from the continent. Is this not a war zone?

After spending the day sightseeing, I needed a drink. Bars tended to group together in clusters, like the storefronts in Chinatown, New York, except they were glitzy, covered in mirrors, brightly colored signs and lights. "Light My Fire," "Reach Out I'll Be There," and "All You Need Is Love" blared. Bargirls dressed in Western clothing lured patrons inside. I walked into a small place that smelled like cigarettes and incense, where the lights and mirrors and statuary gave the feel of some holy place blessed by the Buddha. There were maybe ten patrons sitting or standing at the bar, all men, all Westerners, except for the Asian bartender. I was the only one dressed in fatigues and felt out of place.

Dressed in revealing, tight-fitting skirts and sheaths, the bar girls would engage lonely men with an invitation to buy them a Saigon Tea, a sweet drink served in a double shot glass, or demitasse cup. I had never had a prostitute, and frankly was suspicious. In training, they told us stories about bar girls fronting for the VC. Needless to say, guys stationed in cities like Nha Trang still shacked up with Vietnamese girls for months, and even married them, until it was time to ship home. Many of the girls were left behind. I didn't know whom to believe and hadn't yet gotten used to the idea of paying for sex, but I was curious.

I was attracted to one woman in particular, dressed in the traditional *áo dài,* about five-eight, slender, with high cheekbones and full, sensuous lips. When I saw her hair, the color of dark chocolate and huge blue-gray eyes, I thought she might have been French-Vietnamese. Later I would learn that the Vietnamese looked down on "half-breeds." I couldn't take my eyes off her. When she walked by my table, I gently reached for her arm and must have startled her. She was shy, yet somewhat aloof, indifferent. The scent of Chanel No. 5 overcame me, reminding me of my ex, Lisa. Before I could say anything, she spoke: "Would you like a drink, GI?"

Her voice was warm and mature, like Faye Dunaway in "Bonnie and Clyde," yet she couldn't have been any older than me at 23.

"I'll have a rum and Coke."

She nodded and went to the bar to place the order. It was a strange feeling: a waitress taking my drink order and hers, with the hope that I'd be a customer for a little boom-boom. She sat next to me at the table, just large enough for two drinks and an ashtray.

She brought the cup to her lips momentarily, and looked at me while she sipped. "Where you from, GI?"

"New York; my name's Peter."

She tried to pronounce my name, her sultry voice melting in my ears. "Pee-ter … Pee-ter … Pee-ter."

I took a long sip of my drink. The sweet liquid flowed down my throat, the sensation prickly and smooth and satisfying. The day had been warm, even for late December.

"What's your name?"

"Tuyến."

"That's a pretty name."

She smiled, but seemed embarrassed.

"It means Angel."

Perfect name for a prostitute. I held up my glass in a toast: "To Tuyến; Merry Christmas and good health."

She took a sip, but didn't acknowledge my toast. Then she scoped out the bar, perhaps looking for a regular "companion". She seemed uncomfortable with small talk and wanted to get down to business.

"You speak good English."

"My stepfather has taught me English." She quickly finished her drink.

"Your stepfather?"

She hesitated for a few moments collecting her thoughts. "Do you want to buy me another drink, Peeter?"

I thought for a moment, not sure whether I was ready to follow through with the endplay.

"Do you like me, Peeter?"

I wasn't sure what to say, and I didn't want to scare her away. She intrigued me.

"I'll buy you another drink, but I've never paid for boom-boom before."

She gave me a quizzical look.

"I'm new to this game."

"This no game for me," she shouted.

Indignant, she stormed off and started talking to other patrons.

A few minutes later, I took my drink to the bar and sat next to a heavy, blond civilian with an Australian accent. We talked for a few minutes before he finished his beer and took off. The guy to my other side was an older man, fiftyish, with shorts and a tropical shirt like you'd see in Florida. He sounded like an American, but avoided me. I had no idea what these two guys did for a living. For all I knew, they were doing business with the VC and didn't want to be seen with me.

I sat staring at the bottles on the back bar in front of a mirrored wall, all familiar brands of whiskey, gin, and vodka. Red and blue spotlights cast an eerie glow on my face. I felt trapped inside the mirror looking out, unwelcome and now self-conscious because everyone in the place knew I was a GI. I'd have left, but Tuyến entranced me. I watched her work the patrons. First one guy and then another bought her drinks, but nothing happened. About two hours later, she was sitting alone at a table in the rear, so I went over and asked if she wanted some company. She shrugged her shoulders. "You've Lost That Loving Feeling" was playing on the jukebox. An image of my ex, Lisa, and me dancing at Café Garzone flashed through my mind. I sat next to her.

"Slow night?"

She was staring at the front door of the bar, as if trying to conjure up a customer.

"So … Tuyến? Tell me about yourself."

She glanced my way, but she seemed disinterested. "No. We talk about you."

"Okay. I'm a college dropout. I want to be a doctor, but I was bored with school. My grades were poor because I didn't study. I wasn't motivated. I thought if I had any hope of medical school, I should take some time off and grow up before going back. Then I got drafted and here I am."

She watched my face with interest while I talked. "Do you have girlfriend?"

I shook my head. "No. She dumped me after I went in the army."

She looked perplexed, "Why she do that?"

"I wish I knew. I thought she loved me."

Tuyến shook her head and laughed. "She shows love in funny way."

"Yeah. I don't think her mother approved of me. What could a college dropout going off to war offer her daughter?" The words reverberated as I thought of Lisa, and a wave of sadness and regret swept over me.

"I'm going up to get another rum and Coke. Do you want a tea?"

"I get it for you," she said.

"No," and I went up to the bar. I noticed Tuyến watching me. When I returned, she smiled.

"Thank you, Peter."

"Okay. Now it's your turn to show and tell."

She looked at me in confusion. "Show … tell?"

I laughed. "Show and tell is a figure of speech. It's the way children are taught to share their experiences with the class in elementary school."

"Oh!" She laughed, her face for the first time showing an expression of happiness.

"Tell me about yourself."

She was a student at Saigon National Music School studying European composers and wanted to go to France, but her family couldn't afford to send her. The family had relocated from Saigon a year earlier. Her Vietnamese stepfather was a white-collar government employee and had been transferred to the office in Nha Trang. Her mother, an art teacher, couldn't find work, and was doing laundry at the Special Forces base.

"So, what happened to your father?"

"He was a Capitaine in the French Foreign Legion and met my mother in 1946. He'd send money and see us when he wasn't traveling, but after Dien Bien Phu, he left for an assignment in Morocco and never returned." Her face showed no sign of emotion.

"My mother was very sad. She loved him. I loved him. We never heard from him again."

I reached for her hand and held it tightly. "I'm sorry."

"My stepfather is good man. He provides for my mother and me." She looked down at her hands. "My parents can't afford to send me away to college. This is the only way that I can save enough money. I tried to get job in an office, but because of the way I look, they say I'm better suited to be bar girl."

I watched the curve of her lips as she spoke. I wanted to kiss them, but I kept thinking how easy it would be to be taken in by a VC sympathizer as alluring as Tuyến. She looked up at me, her eyes betraying a deep sadness. It seemed like a high personal price to pay for an education. But then again, how could I understand her predicament, a young man who had been given everything in life, could have gone to any college and studied anything he wanted, but threw it all away? How fitting that I was face to face with my polar opposite, a person who lived in a country at war, had few choices for employment and was willing to sell her body to make her dream a reality. I felt ashamed.

As the evening drifted away, I lost all sense of time. The music made me feel at home, and after too many rum and Cokes, I was in no pain. I really hadn't considered staying at the bar all night, but I was struck by Tuyến. Yes, I wanted to have sex with her, but I felt a deeper connection I hadn't expected.

WE TALKED UNTIL THE bar closed at 0200. I was ready to walk back to the base, but then remembered that it was past base curfew. If the MPs found me, I'd be in trouble. I never thought about the VC and what interest they might have with an unarmed Green Beret at night in their city. I felt like a fool, but Tuyến must have thought otherwise. She told me it would be dangerous walking alone on the streets, and that I should come home with her. I had to agree.

We left the bar through the rear entrance into a dark, narrow alley. Tuyến had a motorbike leaning against the building under a small light fixture. She straddled the seat with her áo dài hiked up over her thighs, and motioned for me to get on the back. It was awkward, as I was so much taller and heavier than her. As I rode with my arms around Tuyến's waist, I could feel her firm belly and smell her perfume. I never liked riding as a passenger on a motorbike, even with a driver larger than me. That evening, I was frightened because the streets were wet and she was going fast, taking corners quickly. We coursed through dark side streets and alleys; the few men we passed looking at me with interest. Perhaps that's why she drove as boldly as she did. I realized how vulnerable I was, perched on the back of that motorbike like one of those huge stuffed animals you win at the county fair. I was thinking that I might have been better off just walking back to base, and was concerned that maybe she was setting me up. But none of those men I saw along the way made a move to stop her, nor did she acknowledge any of them.

Tuyến's home was in a crowded neighborhood on the outskirts of the city. The buildings were sandwiched together, and from a distance looked like a fortress. In the darkness, they were foreboding. I was worried. What if she was taking me to some VC hovel where she'd collect an evening's wages for turning over a US soldier?

Tuyến stowed the motorbike in a narrow alley by the side of her home. The door was in front, and we entered into a parlor. She led me by the hand as we went through two other rooms in darkness on the way to her bedroom. She lit a single votive candle on a corner table, the flickering flame casting a warm glow over stucco walls, red clay tile floor, and a square featherbed in the center of the room. We stood facing one another. She kissed me, touching my face gently, and then smiled as she unbuttoned my fatigue shirt. I slipped it off my shoulders and as it fell to the floor, I embraced her, kissing her deeply. My hands gently caressed her body, the silk of her áo dài smooth against my skin. I stroked her breasts and her head rocked back gently, eyes closed. We stood naked facing one another, then entered a tile shower adjacent to her bedchamber. As the warm water splashed over my body, she washed me gently with a pungent lavender soap, Skillful as a conductor, her hands teased every nerve ending in my body. I lathered her in the soap, my hands following the curves of her exquisite shape, and then we embraced standing under the showerhead. The soft, fragrant towels smelled like her perfume as she dried my body and me hers. When we were finished, she took me by the hand to her bed and in the quiet of the night she made love to me. Afterward, lying in the breadth of my arms, she slept. I lay awake for a time listening to her slow, measured breathing and at once didn't want to go back outside to the war I would soon have to face. Even though I had only met this woman a few hours earlier, I felt as one with her.

The next morning, I was mortified to learn that we had walked through her parents' bedroom on the way to hers. On the way out, we startled them as we scurried past the foot of their bed. I just wanted to bolt out the door and run, but Tuyến grabbed my hand and calmed me down.

It was 0830, and I was late for formation. I had no idea where the base was, or how long it would take to get there. I told Tuyến that I had to go. Standing in front of her home, she took both of my hands in hers and began to pull them toward her body nervously, as if she didn't want me to leave, then she kissed me and began to cry.

"Will I see you again, Peter?"

I wanted to see her, but I'd be shipping out in a matter of days. Then I'd be over 400 klicks away somewhere in Tactical Zone III. I held Tuyến's face in my hands.

"Please stop crying," I said, as I stroked the tears from her cheeks. "I'll see you again before I ship out."

I bent to kiss her and she wrapped her arms around my shoulders tightly and wouldn't let go.

I whispered: "I promise."

As I walked through the neighborhoods of the city on the way back to base, my gut ached. I kept thinking about how trapped she must feel. Then I realized that I had ripped her off. In my haste to leave, I'd forgotten to pay her. She had never said a word. She had given herself to me without precondition. Not only had I taken advantage of her, but I had given her hope. I was disgusted with myself. I wasn't much better than the Frenchman who was her father.

Later I learned the VC paid a $200 bounty for the ear or dog tags of a Green Beret. It didn't make me feel any better about what I did. I may have owed her my life.

Saigon

I received orders to ship out the day after Christmas; first to Saigon, then on to Bien Hoa. I outprocessed from Nha Trang and relaxed the day before leaving. As I lay on my bunk that afternoon, I couldn't get Tuyến out of my mind. I wanted to see her again, to hold her, to feel the warmth of her body against mine. I was sure her parents were interested in the American who slept with their daughter, because she told me she never brought customers home. I couldn't understand their customs and culture. How could a parent allow a daughter to sell her body? Was I Tuyến's ticket out of Vietnam? Had her mother been a prostitute, and did she fall in love with a soldier? Why were the Americans any different than the French? They colonized the Vietnamese, conscripted them in forced labor camps to toil on French-owned rubber plantations and otherwise treated them as indentured servants, second-class citizens in their own country. Frenchmen impregnated their daughters and went home, leaving them behind, and we did the same. I was confused and depressed, unsure of what to expect in this strange new country.

The C-7 Caribou aircraft took off with three passengers and climbed quickly to about 7,500 feet, leveled off, out of range of anything but antiaircraft rockets. The drone of the plane's engines was hypnotic. The scenery was breathtaking, an endless patchwork of the now familiar greens and browns, farmers' fields and rice paddies terraced and bermed, jungle, forests, rubber plantations, and the South China seacoast. Villages were groups of buildings gathered together as if in an embrace, thatched and tiled roofs in community, paradise through a fish-eye lens. As we approached Saigon, I marveled at the sheer size and sprawl of this metropolis bordered by the Saigon River. I was told that the population of the city was two million, plus another million if you included the 20-klick surrounding suburban area. We landed in a corner of Tan Sun Nhut airbase reserved for military aircraft. A deuce-and-a-half picked us up for the ride to Camp Goodwin.

We arrived amid the crush of midday traffic. An eight-foot tall, stone and wrought iron wall with an ornate iron gate surrounded the compound. It was a villa left over from the French colonial era, commandeered by the South Vietnamese government after the fall of Dien Bien Phou, and loaned to the US. The camp was a way station that offered respite for Special Forces operatives. After checking in with the Officer of the Day, I headed for the shower. Traveling anywhere in Vietnam was unpleasant. In the dry season, dirt and perspiration became a poultice on the skin; during monsoon, the poultice became a mudpack. I have never looked forward to a shower more than while in Vietnam; there were none out in the boonies and few at A-Camps.

Saigon was headquarters for the US military establishment. Vietnam had been at war for 20 years, first with the French, and after 1954, the National Liberation Front, the NLF. The city and surrounding suburbs were crowded with over a half million refugees from the war-ravaged central and northern provinces, most said to be NLF sympathizers. Saigon was considered a safe city, except for occasional sabotage or shooting in the streets. Soldiers from the Republic of Vietnam (South Vietnam), the US and its allies walked the streets and patrolled its roads. I still didn't feel safe.

I spent the afternoon and evening touring a section of the city within walking distance of Goodwin. It was a mix of elegant French colonial buildings and dilapidated structures that you might see in a Mexican border town: shop stalls, grimy buildings and apartments with the first floor converted into makeshift shops. Residential areas were a hodgepodge of apartments, estates, pigpens and single-family homes. Saigon had the cosmopolitan feel of an international city, with a mix of nationalities, like London or Montreal, but disheveled and tarnished. The French attempt to turn the city into the Paris of the Orient appeared to have fallen short. It had a worn, used-up look, perhaps from the vicissitudes of tropical weather. That and the ubiquitous debris made it look shabby and unkempt. Nevertheless, the French influence still existed, with many older Vietnamese fluent in the language.

A French bakery next to a noodle stand got my attention, and I went inside. The French bread and pastries looked every bit as good as those available in New York City, and indeed the crullers were outstanding. In fact, the proprietor, a stocky middle-aged Vietnamese man who spoke good English, had trained in Paris.

The crowds were not unlike those in American cities, people going on about their business—men dressed in business suits or white short-sleeve dress shirts and slacks; women most often wore the traditional áo dài or business suits. There was much evidence of poverty and homelessness, the distinction between the haves and have-nots apparent. Disfigured people begged in front of magnificent colonial buildings, limbless, blind or horribly burned, some soldiers, but most were the collateral damage of war, women and old men whose farms, perhaps, had been destroyed in a B-52 strike or whose villages had been napalmed. This was my introduction to the innocents of war, and it made me sick to my stomach. They never talked about this in training, either.

Saigon was a study in contrasts: strange yet familiar, tense yet relaxed, lonely yet exuberant. Well-dressed people and soldiers shared city sidewalks. Men on bicycles pedaled amid choking vehicular traffic, defying death. Coke bottles and Marlboro cigarettes were displayed in a sidewalk shop alongside hanging smoked duck and live chickens. Daytime Saigon seemed a well-behaved prude compared with nighttime Saigon. The city was full of life after dark and it all revolved around sex. I toured a few of the clubs on a street they called "The Strip". Most of them had live music, all contemporary Western culture, with musicians mimicking the real artists. There was a group that looked and sounded just like the Beatles except for their Asian faces and slight bodies. After several drinks, I was hard-pressed to tell the difference. The bargirls dyed and coiffed their hair like western women, and dressed in mini-skirts and boots, or revealing evening wear. I bought a few Saigon Teas that evening, but soon lost interest. I headed back to Goodwin early, with Tuyến on my mind.

The next morning, I caught a jeep to Bien Hoa, a suburb of Saigon. It was a 30-klick drive, and traffic in the morning was light. The city, with a population of roughly 200,000, was home to a large US Air Force base and Special Forces headquarters for Tactical Zone III. After checking in at the C-Team, I went to the mess hall for chow, followed by a 1400-hour meeting with Sergeant Major Mills. His office was crammed into the end of a mobile home. There was barely enough room to move between the file cabinets along the wall and his desk, which was piled high with manila folders.

Mills was the top NCO at headquarters. His jungle fatigues were clean but disheveled. He needed a haircut. I guess I expected that he'd look the part of the senior noncom, but this was Vietnam, not Fort Bragg. He had a firm jaw and penetrating blue eyes as he looked at me then down at a folder on his desk.

"McShane, welcome to III Corps."

He reached across the desk to shake my hand.

He seemed anxious, as if he was afraid I'd ask him for a favor, like being assigned to a quiet dispensary job at the C-Team. The thought never occurred to me.

"We can sure use your help. We need you to set up a regional hospital down on the coast at Long Hai." The words lingered in my ears.

I'm a lowly Spec 4, a junior medic with no field experience, and you want me to set up a hospital? It didn't make sense to me.

He went on to say that I'd be assigned to a special purpose A-Team called the Mobile Strike Force, Mike Force for short, team A-302, whose base camp was located on the shores of the South China Sea near the village of Long Hai, about 70 klicks from Saigon.

"You've got 2,500 Cambodian and Chinese Nûng strikers and their families living with you, and your dispensary is not adequate to the task of caring for them. You'll also serve the villagers from Long Hái."

As he talked, it occurred to me that maybe I had just lucked out. This would be as close to a stateside assignment as I'd ever get in Nam. I daydreamed about relaxing on the beach on my days off.

"Is the building already set up?"

"No. You'll be starting from scratch. We'll get the building materials ordered and you can use the army engineers that are working on your airstrip to build the hospital. When you get down to Long Hái, tell Lew Brown what we talked about, okay?

"Sure, Sergeant Major."

I remember walking out of that meeting elated that I probably wouldn't need any of my infantry training. I had a few beers that evening in the NCO club to celebrate with other troopers who appeared to be less fortunate than me, given their destinations to A-Camps near the Cambodian border.

The next day, I boarded a chopper for the 30-minute flight to Long Hái, and we headed toward the South China Seacoast. We frequently changed direction and altitude to confuse any potential ground-based attack. As we approached the camp, the beach came into view. Hotels and villas dotted the shoreline. I could see swimmers in the water enjoying the day. The sky was royal blue and cloudless. The camp was right on the beach, 500 meters from the water's edge. The coast road separated the camp from the beach where the striker encampment and improvised airstrip were located.

Master Sergeant Lew Brown, *a.k.a.* "Top," the Mike Force Team Leader, grabbed my duffel and helped me off the chopper. We exchanged greetings and then he told me to get a field rig together, because I was going out on a mission in about two hours.

"The sergeant major told me I'd be setting up a regional hospital."

Top laughed.

"McShane, the hospital has been on the drawing board since we relocated from Bien Hoa in July. I'd love for you to spend time caring for our Cambodes, Nûngs, and the villagers, but we're short staffed, and in a month, we're losing our senior medic, so you'll be the only medic on the team. I need you in the field."

I was confused and wondered what the fuck was going on. He added that getting supplies for the A-Camp for day-to-day living and operations was tough enough; acquiring the resources to build a hospital was a real long shot. He wasn't kidding. I had trouble finding enough gear to make up a field harness, not to mention a modern weapon. There weren't enough M-16s to go around, so I borrowed a teammate's, who was out of country on R&R. The alternative was a WWII vintage M-2 carbine, which was what our strikers carried. I remember feeling thankful that I had smuggled that Browning pistol into country.

The Mike Force was a double A-Team special operations task force organized by Tactical Zone in Vietnam, one for each of four Zones. The Mike Force had a dual mission. We were inserted whenever an A-Camp in our district needed backup. If a Camp was under siege, we went to the rescue. Our second role was to harass and interdict the enemy, *a.k.a.* recon—clandestine reconnaissance missions into Cambodia, which was officially off-limits to US personnel; we traveled with no identification other than a Mike Force patch on our uniform, and a red, white, and blue scarf around our neck. A majority of the eighteen A-Camps in our Tactical Zone were near the border.

I was in the air on the way to my first operation before I realized it. The hospital and the image of me as a healer became a dream long forgotten. The fantasy of just saving lives vaporized like a morning jungle mist. I was pissed. The sergeant major lied to me. How could he not know the staffing situation at Long Hái? And there was a lot more that he didn't tell me. Years later I learned my team was one of the most highly decorated small units during the Vietnam War. From May 1966 to March 1967, nine months before my arrival, with seldom more than nine men operational at any one time, team members were awarded one Congressional Medal of Honor, three Distinguished Service Crosses, twelve Silver Stars, eleven Bronze Stars for Valor, and seventeen Purple Hearts, eight of which were posthumous.

Devil's Triangle

The CH-47 Chinook lifted off with a third of our Cambodian striker company, an ARVN Special Forces advisor with his translator, me, and a teammate. Aluminum fuselage ribs gave shape to the cavernous belly of this beast. The noise inside the chopper was deafening. I could feel the engines vibrate from my boots to the top of my skull.

I squatted on the floor with the strikers, next to Staff Sergeant Bill Williams, our weapons team leader and a two-tour Nam vet. Bill was a lifer, in Special Forces for 11 years going for 20. He didn't look like a trained killer, but what does a trained killer look like, anyway? He was slender with glasses and so was I, except he had a prominent Adam's apple. Green as a Granny Smith, I was reluctant to ask any questions for fear of betraying my naiveté. Just out of training, I had no fucking idea what I was doing. Good with Band-Aids; it turned out that's all my teammates cared about, anyway.

Williams and I were in a sea of strikers. I felt self-conscious. They all looked so young, so small. If there was any feature that stuck out, it was their demeanor: always in a good mood, smiling, laughing, and joking with one another. I wondered if they were talking about me. Williams watched me scan the crowd.

"What sort of fighters are they?"

"Don't let their playful ways fool you. These guys are brutal. They hate communism."

"Where are we headed, Bill?"

"Devil's Triangle." The words sent a shiver down my spine. He saved me the embarrassment of asking more questions, adding that we'd be running joint search-and-clear operations with the 25th Infantry Division and an ARVN battalion.

Part of a large sweep through the region, it was loaded with enemy troops in what appeared to be a buildup of forces, perhaps for a major offensive. It was early January 1968.

"My bet is we'll be running operations in several rubber plantations. They're spread throughout Tay Ninh and surrounding provinces." It was hard to hear Williams over the whine of the engines.

The pungent smell of burning aircraft fuel reminded me of the kerosene space heater I used once on a construction project back home.

"What is the Devil's Triangle?"

"It's the area between Cambodia and Tay Ninh City, Routes 22 to the west and 13 to the east, North Vietnamese Army resupply routes. Those roads link the Ho Chi Minh Trail with Saigon. Ever hear of the 'Iron Triangle'?"

I shook my head.

"It lies between Tay Ninh and Saigon and was a Viet Minh stronghold during the French war. Now it's an NVA stronghold. The Big Red One, the 173rd Airborne, and the 25th Infantry, to name a few, have tried to kick them out. Relentless B-52 strikes haven't worked. Nothing has worked." He paused for a minute, his lips drawn back in a sneer.

"All we've done is piss off the locals, bombing and burning their villages, killing their families. Anyway, it's been hot up here for months. The Camp at Loc Ninh on Route 13 was almost overrun with tanks last month. We lost a lot of guys and our Nûng Company was sliced to bits."

"Tanks?"

"Yeah, man. Tanks. And they kicked our ass with artillery fired from bases in Cambodia."

This was all news to me. Why didn't they tell us this shit in training?

"This your first tour, McShane?"

"Yeah," I responded in a casual tone. I wondered if he could tell I was scared shitless. "The C-Team Sergeant Major told me I would be setting up a regional hospital in Long Hái. I thought I had reason to celebrate, you know, like I wouldn't be seeing any combat. Top Brown gave me the news of this operation as I got off the chopper from Bien Hoa about two hours ago. I haven't even unpacked my duffel."

Williams chuckled and shook his head. "Medics are in short supply."

"What do you mean?"

"We're supposed to have four, now we have two. There's Sgt. Glenn and you, and Glenn's tour ends in three weeks. McShane ... you're the man."

"How come we're in short supply?"

"You're all getting greased! Normally, you newbies would be stationed at the C-Team or a B-Team for a few months to get your bearings, and then you'd be assigned to a quiet A-Camp. Congratulations, you just moved to the head of the class. This is the hottest A-Team in Zone III, and we're on the way to the hottest area."

"That's great," I said in my best gung ho, while I could feel my stomach churn. My hands began to sweat.

While we talked, several of the strikers were touching me on the shoulder and arms, smiling and nodding, gestures of friendship. They addressed me as Bác Sĩ, Vietnamese for Doctor.

I couldn't see out of the chopper's portholes without standing, but I could tell that we must be approaching a landing zone; the pilot cut airspeed. The deal was that we'd land at the Quan Loi Plantation airstrip long enough to regroup and board Hueys for the trip to our LZ somewhere west of the town of An Loc.

"I hate these Shithooks," yelled Williams, who stood up, preparing to run down the chopper's exit ramp.

"They churn up too much sand and dust. I'd rather transport in a C-130 or a Caribou any day."

The chopper touched down hard, bounced twice and slipped to the left in a gust of wind. I lost my balance and would have fallen to the floor had I not been boxed in among our strikers. They smirked watching me as I struggled to regain my footing.

Once on the ground, Captain Nigel Lauder, our team CO, pulled us all together. He had arrived moments earlier on the first chopper with four other teammates, including Sergeant First Class Joe Stevens, another lifer on his third tour.

"We'll head out at 1500. Our LZ is west of the Xacam rubber plantation. Route 13 runs through it, with the town of An Loc at the north end, and the Quan Loi Plantation, where we are now, five klicks to the east. We have 10 Hueys at our disposal. Chances are that the LZ will be hot, so once on the ground head for cover in the jungle on the west side of the LZ. We'll run a quick search and clear, then set up bivouac for the evening. Our mission will last for a week, with the objective of driving Charlie out of the rubber trees and toward the regular army guys located here." He pointed to an area on the map just west of An Loc.

Lauder, plus six Americans providing tactical support to the strikers would lead the operation. I'd be the seventh, the medic along for the ride. We had a couple of hours before liftoff, and I walked over to where Williams was standing. We headed off the airstrip, a long patch of dusty red earth cut out of a golf course that had been built by the Terres Rouges Rubber Company, which owned several plantations in the area. At the edge of the course was a clubhouse, a French provincial mansion with a red tile roof and a second story balcony with floor to ceiling French doors. As we walked by the front of the building, I wondered at the magnificence of the place, the golf course and all, in the middle of the jungle. A white fence surrounded a courtyard in front. To the right was an in-ground pool bordered by tall white columns and a huge trellis draped with flowering vines. Bougainvillea and other fragrant flowers filled the compound, which was shaded by palm and banyan trees. An attractive Vietnamese woman, dressed in a chartreuse ào dái, was sitting in a rattan chair on the terrace adjacent to the pool. She was watching several Caucasian children frolic in the water. I could see a rotund, middle-aged Caucasian male standing at the edge of the pool several feet from the Vietnamese woman. When the fat cat saw Williams and me dressed in our tiger fatigues and armed with M-16s, he snorted at us as if to say, "Get off of my plantation."

"Looks like boss man doesn't like us, Pete."

I wondered what that guy was doing there. He didn't appear concerned about his safety or the well-being of the children. I thought about all the people I had seen on the streets in Saigon, oblivious to the war, and wondered what I was missing.

We headed back to the LZ to rest before lifting off. Quan Loi was home to a Howitzer artillery battalion that supported the 25th Infantry, as well as our A-Camps in the area. They'd be on call if we ran into trouble. Their base was one klick the other side of the airstrip. Beyond that was a Montagnard Village, an ethnic group of primitive people who lived simple lives among the Vietnamese. They were friendly, anticommunist, and sympathetic to our cause. Some of our A-Camps relied on the "Yards" to staff their mercenary companies, much like our Cambodes and Nûngs.

Williams and I climbed into the first Huey, its blades churning up the awful red dust that was as fine as talcum powder. We lifted off gaining altitude quickly. Riding in one of these choppers was a delight compared with Shithooks, because there was no sheet metal or doors to obstruct our view. Door gunners provided cover for hot LZs, but that didn't stop the enemy from taking pot shots. It was a job I didn't want. I'd take the confines of the triple-canopy jungle any day. At least there was cover, a place to hide. I sat with my back against a bulkhead at the edge of the cockpit. The pungent afternoon air buffeted my body as we cruised at treetop level. The jungle canopy beyond the landing skids below rushed by in patches of red and green and brown like the pelt of some massive creature. The colors were more vivid than training missions in North Carolina. It was a panoramic movie in Technicolor, like *Around the World in 80 Days* or *Giant*. The stench of rotting vegetation and the acrid smoke of cooking fires were an ever-present reminder that it was not a movie, but here and now. This was Charlie's home.

A few minutes later the chopper began to throttle back, losing altitude—we were approaching the LZ. I braced myself for what was to come. In practice, we assumed that the enemy would be there waiting for us, guns ablazing. I began to tense up, adrenaline coursing through my arteries and veins. Colors seemed more vivid, the sound of the chopper blades louder, the movie scene on fast-forward. I could see the ground come up fast. Within seconds the door gunners blasted away with their M-60s. I couldn't tell whether Charlie was firing back at us. The chopper bounced on the ground. Will I get shot before reaching cover? Will this be the end of my tour—my life? Hovering in the prop wash of dust and debris, I jumped with my M-16 at the ready and ran through tall grass and brush toward the western edge of the LZ, about 100 meters away. I wondered whether I'd have to hit the ground at some point to escape a fusillade of enemy bullets. Running as hard as I could, it felt like I wasn't gaining ground. The tree line wasn't getting any closer. My heart raced and I felt trapped, in a dream-like state, evil gaining on me, surrounding me, but I couldn't get to safety. In the noise and confusion, I couldn't tell if the enemy was shooting at me.

I ran and ran and ran, and just as I reached the edge of the jungle, there was Williams, sitting up and facing me, smiling.

"McShane—no Charlie!"

Out of breath and relieved, I collapsed on the ground next to him.

"Shit, after what Lauder said, I was expecting the worst. I couldn't tell whether there was any shooting other than the door gunners." I felt like a jerk.

"Bad intel. Charlie doesn't shoot until we're all on the ground. You would have known it. Don't feel bad. It happens to all of us."

We rendezvoused, split into four columns and reconnoitered the jungle to the west of the LZ. I was in the column behind Lauder, hypervigilant, jumpy with anticipation. I had visions of Charlie leaping out from behind a stand of bamboo, lunging at me with fixed bayonet. I saw patches on the ground that looked like punji pits. Every sound startled me. Thumps sounded like the launching of a 60mm mortar. Someone is watching me. Someone wants to kill me. But when I watched the other Americans, they seemed at ease. I wondered how they could be so relaxed. All I could think about was being captured. If I were paraded in front of villagers locked in a bamboo cage, would they take out their frustration with Americans on me? What if Charlie threatened to cut off my dick? Would I cave?

We pitched camp about a klick from the LZ. Stevens and one of my other teammates set up a perimeter within which our company would bivouac. The strikers were responsible for our security. Night watch was set up and enforced by their squad leaders.

We gathered in groups around common cooking fires. The strikers brought live chickens and bags of rice with them on operations, the birds stowed in burlap bags to keep them quiet. Spices were either carried dry, or the men foraged for them in the jungle. I was curious about their food after talking with Williams.

"McShane, if you like spicy, try it. Frankly, it gives me the shits."

LRRP rations, several variants of freeze-dried chicken or beef, were our standard-issue meal—just add water, heat it, and slop it down. It was tasteless gruel that had to be doctored with Tabasco or an onion in order to make it edible. The strikers loved LRRPs because they came with candy-coated gum and cigarettes. That first evening, I traded mine for a bowl of chicken soup with rice on the side. Five strikers and I sat around the fire, while one of them ladled soup into my canteen cup. They watched in childlike anticipation as I put the cup to my lips. It was spicy hot but delicious, an unexpected treat. They must have put extra chilies in my soup expecting a reaction, but they didn't get one. They were surprised when I asked for seconds. There were a few Cambodian dishes that I didn't like, fish eye soup being at the top of that list. It was difficult to keep my appetite with the eyes of half a dozen hapless fish, origins unknown, staring at me. At least I had seen the chickens alive before the meal.

After chow, Lauder huddled with us and we planned our strategy for the next few days. I shot the shit with Stevens and Williams for an hour afterward, until it began to get dark. I was curious about Lauder. He was a handsome, confident man in his early thirties with a muscular build and spoke with a mild Spanish accent.

"What's the story about Lauder?"

"Knows his shit, seen a lot of action," said Stevens.

"He's Cuban," added Williams. "He fought for us with the CIA in the Bay of Pigs. He was a paratrooper in Battista's army. After the failed operation, he did a tour with the US Marines and then joined us. He's a warrior."

I didn't know whether that was good or bad, but I was comforted because it sounded like he was experienced.

The next morning came early, with a hint of the sun at around 0500. The strikers milled around our campsite, getting their fires started for the morning meal. The plan for the week was to push the Xacam Plantation from West to East, starting at the northern end. We'd line up our company north to south, spacing ourselves 10 to 12 meters apart, and drive a section of it every day, about a five-klick hike. We left our base camp at 0630. The first thing I noticed about the jungle was how dark it was during the day. Triple canopy growth all but shut out the sun's rays. Vegetation at ground level could grow six feet high, with climbing vines and small trees growing to 25 feet, and both overshadowed by tall trees growing over 50 feet tall, veritable walls and ceiling. It was eerie, like dusk in the morning, and damp like Uwharrie after a rain. It smelled like rotting vegetation. The ground was choked with plant life, vines spiraling up tree trunks and hanging off branches. Wildlife was everywhere—tigers, antelope, deer, monkeys, pheasants, vampire bats, snakes, and outsized insects: grasshoppers, weevils, scorpions, spiders, and mosquitos that carried the malaria parasite.

Within an hour, we had only reached the western edge of Xacam, which was less than a klick away. It was warm, 80 degrees plus, and the humidity oppressive. I was drenched, and it was only 0730. After a short break, we walked into the plantation between trees lined up in neat rows. It looked as if it had been several years since the property was cultivated. I'd never seen a rubber tree. They were slender, the typical trunk not more than a foot in diameter, the gnarled bark variegated brown to chalky white and stained with latex. Large oval leaves came three on a stem. They didn't look like any of the trees back home. Some of the trees were damaged, perhaps from previous firefights or bombing. Trails cut between the rows of trees, used to haul out the liquid latex, were clogged with elephant grass four to six feet high. It was a perfect place for an ambush.

We humped until 1200, stopping to take a chow break next to a small abandoned village tucked in among the rubber trees. A rundown bungalow stood in front of a row of buildings that looked like barracks. Williams walked up to my side.

"How you doing?"

I was sopping wet with perspiration and exhausted. "Okay, I guess."

He looked me over. "You'll get used to it."

We sat at the base of a rubber tree on the edge of a clearing where I could see the bungalow. "What happened to this village?"

"The French built these camps in the 1920s. They shipped in laborers from all over Vietnam to clear the jungles and plant the trees. That bungalow over there was where the overseer lived."

I glanced around at what was left of the village.

"Looks like no one's been here in years."

"Not since our little war began. We started poking around here in the early 1960s."

After eating a LRRP, I grabbed my M-16 and walked over to the buildings to take a closer look. The barracks were rather primitive, made out of wood and bamboo, with corrugated metal roofs. There were dilapidated, screened windows open to the weather and doors torn off their hinges. I walked across what must have been a courtyard. A rusty flagpole teetered in the humidity, its base surrounded, as if propped up, by a circle of white stones. The bungalow looked like comfortable quarters, with a roof that overhung the sides of the building, glass windows with screens and a large porch in front with a hanging swing. Behind the bungalow was a small building, perhaps 15 feet square with two small windows near the soffit, each covered with a cast iron grate, maybe a jail or holding cell. I wondered who the overseer had been—a Frenchman or a mixed-race French-Vietnamese? Inside the building were rusted ankle irons and chains, and large eyebolts in the wall timbers. I walked back over where Williams was leaning against a tree.

"There's a jail or holding cell over behind the bungalow. What's up with that?"

"The French brutalized and exploited the Vietnamese. These labor camps were as close to human servitude as you could get short of slavery. Laborers died by the thousands carving the plantations out of the jungle. These rubber trees were fertilized with the decaying bodies of dead laborers—capitalism at its finest."

"My God. How long was this going on?"

"For years, until the communists organized the workers in the early 1930s and conditions improved."

In training, there was little detail about the struggles of the Vietnamese people. My image had been of helpless, downtrodden, lackadaisical gooks, people not in control of their destiny who needed to be liberated. As I looked at the jail, I couldn't help but think there must have been much suffering here at the hands of the French. And how is that any different now that the Americans are here to "liberate" them? As long as we're here, there will be no jobs tending to the rubber trees. There will be no peace. Are we any better than the French?

We headed out at 1300 and by 1800 had made it to within a klick of An Loc. I was tense throughout the afternoon, listening to the crunching of vegetation beneath my feet, waiting for all hell to break loose. But it didn't. We decided to bivouac in the plantation that evening.

THE NEXT TWO DAYS trudging through the rubber plantation, I found myself daydreaming, drifting in thought, thinking about drinking an ice-cold beer, or swimming in the ocean. What is Lisa doing—is she happy? Are we really done, or is she just upset that I joined the army? I wasn't preoccupied with the thought of getting killed any more. I was hot and sweaty and drained. Had I reached equilibrium between the fear of death and the desire to live, the fine line between this world and the next? I didn't care. I just wanted the day to pass. I wanted all my days in Vietnam to pass. I hated it here. I wanted a break, and I'd only just begun my tour.

I snapped out of that addictive stupor in a hurry around 1000 the following morning. AK-47 fire came in on us from about 40 meters out. It was localized near my section of the column, maybe a squad-sized force of 10 soldiers from the sound of it. I hit the ground and was swallowed in vegetation. Visibility was poor in the plantation; we couldn't see Charlie. There was nothing to shoot at. Our strikers were firing their M-2s like crazy, unloading bullet after bullet into the trees and elephant grass, unable to see the enemy, unable to see anything. Lauder looked at his topographical map, grabbed the radio and called Quan Loi Artillery with map coordinates. Two minutes later a 155mm Howitzer marking round zoomed in, sounding like a rocket ship about to crash, and hit the ground about 100 meters in front of us. The explosion was deafening, followed by a shock wave that just about lifted me off the ground. A dust and dirt cloud followed. My ears buzzed. I felt as if someone had cupped my ears and slapped my face. I checked for broken parts, but all was intact. It took a few seconds to regain my focus. Rifle fire had stopped. Lauder radioed to walk the shelling further in about 10 meters and fire three for effect. The rounds hit and I could feel the concussive impact on my body. Dirt rained from overhead. I could hear the shrapnel striking the trees, whipping through elephant grass near me. I hugged the ground as hard as I could but couldn't hide. Thank God I didn't get hit. The awesome power of the bombs was frightening, yet I had an overwhelming feeling of relief and euphoria. How could anything live through that? The battlefield was choked with thick, blue smoke. The acrid smell of cordite burnt my nostrils, but I was safe. We were safe.

Lauder organized a party to search for dead and wounded. As I walked slowly to where the shells had hit, it looked like the ground had just gotten a haircut—it was mowed clean. There were four craters carved out of scorched earth, trees shattered and uprooted. The ground smoldered and stunk of rot. We canvassed a 50-meter radius looking for corpses and body parts in the trees and on the ground, any sign of the enemy. We found nothing. No evidence that anyone had been there.

Long Hải

Our Long Hải base camp was a sandbox situated on the shores of the South China Sea. When I arrived in late December of 1967, combat engineers had built structures to serve as team house, bunkroom, dispensary, storage, and barracks for our strikers. All single-story wood construction, the foundations were floating concrete pads. Sided in clapboards, there were windowless openings covered with shutters and screens to keep out sand fleas and mosquitoes. The engineers were finishing a short landing strip capable of handling helicopters and small aircraft, like Caribou for troop movements, or single-engine Cessnas for aerial observation, FAOs. By the end of January, their work was completed.

The team house measured approximately 18 by 40 feet, divided into two rooms: a kitchen and an all-purpose meeting/dining/living room. The kitchen was a professional setup like ones in the restaurants I had worked in during college, with a range, double oven, refrigerator, and ice machine. We had sinks with running water, thanks to a 300-gallon tank perched atop a tower behind the building. We took meals at a large table that also served for team meetings, or we'd sit at the bar, which was about 15 feet long, complete with cold beer and soda, whiskey, gin, vodka, and assorted liquors. The living room doubled as a movie theater with enough chairs for the team and any visitors. We often had guests for dinner and drinks, whether it was our ARVN counterparts, local government dignitaries, or SF operatives traveling through. Aussies from the armored contingent east of the village of Long Hái were frequent visitors.

Five hundred meters to the south of the camp entrance was the seacoast. The local road from Vũng Tàu, about 26 klicks away, passed by our front gate. Our striker encampment was across the road where their families lived in hundreds of ramshackle sheds, joined together like the segments of a giant earthworm. There were several rows of these structures arranged side by side, and you could walk among the hooches feeling like you were in one contiguous building.

The camp was well fortified, with a bermed perimeter, rows of concertina, machine-gun emplacements, fougas drums, and Claymores. It was safe despite the fact that the nearby Long Hái Mountains were infested with VC. We ran limited patrols in and around the area, and knew that it was a VC stronghold, but they never struck us. We'd trap them in ambushes, and they'd retaliate with a few mortar rounds that would hit outside our perimeter, but they didn't have the manpower to mount any serious campaign. Beside our contingent of 1,500 strikers, B-36 was next door, and their mobile guerilla force numbered over 1,000 strikers. In addition, the Aussies had tanks and armored vehicles. The VC were smart enough to leave a sleeping giant alone.

Life while standing down at camp between operations was as good as it could get, but boring. We had sheets on our bunks. Maids washed our clothes. Routines handling morning sick call, moving supplies from storage to the striker mess hall or ammo dump helped to break the monotony, but by 1200, most of the chores were done. My job as medic was to see to the sanitation needs of the compound. That meant burning the shit from our latrine when it got full. While the engineers were in camp, we burned about once a week. I don't know what was worse—the rancid smell of decaying fecal matter, or the smell of it roasting in diesel fuel.

No one on the team preferred base camp life, not after a field operation—on edge for days at a time, hypervigilant, waiting for the break of gunfire or the thump of an enemy mortar round. And when it happened, it was an adrenaline rush. Life in the jungle was 90 percent waiting for something to happen, and it was easy to get distracted, lost in thought, thinking about how hot and uncomfortable you were, or what your girlfriend was doing back home. Then you'd snap out of it, reminding yourself that at any moment Charlie might attack. When he did, you hoped you could do your job and survive the chaos.

Lee Chang, our Chinese chef, fed us well. In a stroke of genius, we had hired him away from a hotel in Saigon. Our meals were anything but routine: beef bourguignon, breaded pork chops, steak au poivre, and all the seafood we wanted. He made yeast breads, baguettes, and the best pastry desserts I'd ever eaten. We left it up to Chang to source much of our fresh food locally. The list of chow available from the commissary was limited, but we were able to scrounge all the beef, chicken, and pork we wanted.

The downtime at Long Hái often meant an overnight or a weekend in Vũng Tàu. It was a major port and in-country R&R center. It had nice hotels, bars and restaurants, and was considered safe because of the significant US military presence there. We had a deuce and-a-half going in at least twice a week to pick up supplies. When I was in camp, I was the guy who did the run, since I was lowest-ranking soldier. The highway was busy with local traffic, primarily Lambros and motor bikes, but also military vehicles and sedans from Saigon traveling to resorts along the seacoast. The VC would landmine the road and whenever traffic backed up, it was either an accident or a crater from an antitank mine. I ran the road behind a large vehicle whenever possible, leaving enough distance between us to protect my deuce and-a-half.

The military maintained a maze of warehouses in Vũng Tàu at the port. Anything you could imagine was available: military equipment, appliances, furniture, sporting goods, movie projectors, guitars, sheet music, and everything in between. A typical stop might include two or three different warehouses and take the better part of a day. Foodstuffs, soft drinks, and beer were in the commissary warehouse. I'd drive up to the appropriate loading dock and present a requisition form signed by one of our team officers. The NCO on duty would tell me how long it would take to put up the order and I'd come back to find everything palletized and loaded on my truck. This process often took a couple of hours per warehouse, so I had time to kill. I'd putz around the base, stop in the PX, buy film or toothpaste, or get a haircut. If I had more time, I'd go outside the gate, where there were dozens of stores, restaurants, and shops along the street leading to the warehouse complex. I'd grab a bowl of noodles or soup from a street vendor, buy a beer at one of the bars, or get a steam bath.

I got to know the supply NCO, Sergeant Stoner, and after filling my order for a film projector one day, he asked me if we needed anything special.

"What do you mean, Sarge?"

"Like a TV, an air conditioner, or fridge?"

"Nah, we're okay with that stuff. What else do you have?"

He thought for a minute, scratching his chin.

"Hey, where did you say your camp was located?"

"Long Hái, on the beach just up the road."

"The beach, huh."

"Yeah."

"Come with me," he said, and we walked over to another loading bay. Tucked in the corner was a Boston Whaler with twin 40-horse Evinrudes. I almost dropped my jaw, but tried not to look too anxious. Having grown up near Lake Ontario and in and out of boats all my life, I thought this would be perfect; we could water ski.

"I don't know. We spend most of our time in the field."

"Yeah, but think of the trouble you could get into once you're back to base."

Stoner laughed, shaking his head up and down, his eyes bulging out of his head,

"Yeah, man. You guys could get into serious trouble at those resorts—hit and run!"

He continued laughing. This guy was good, a primo salesman. I was hooked. All I had to do was figure out how to make a deal happen.

"What do you need, Sarge?"

He thought for a minute, but I knew he had something in mind. Anything collectable from the field had a strong market with the Legs in the rear. They never saw any action, and these goodies would make them look like combat veterans once they were back home on the block. Sarge could sell this stuff and make a fortune.

"How about half a dozen AKs and Montagnard crossbows, maybe some captured NVA stuff. Whataya got?" he said.

"Let me take a look around camp and I'll bring some gear next time I come in."

That evening over a few beers with my teammates, I introduced the concept of having a ski boat at our disposal, and everyone thought it was a great idea. Next subject was taking an inventory of captured materiel. The Montagnard crossbows were in good supply; we routinely traded tiger stripe fatigues, Mike Force patches and scarves for crossbows and bracelets with our SF brethren in the highlands, home to the Montagnard. We had a room full of

AKs, pistols, submachine guns, mortars, rocket-propelled grenades, uniforms, helmets, and knives.

After the next field operation, Williams and I took the deuce-and-a-half into Vũng Tàu and closed the ski boat deal. It cost us five AKs, six crossbows, and a couple of Chicom SKSs. Bingo. Stoner had his lackeys remove the two engines and they loaded the boat in the back of the truck, placing it on four old truck tires. The motors fit between the tires and the side wall of the truck. He threw in a pair of water skis and tow rope, a gas can, and a gallon of two-cycle motor oil. We headed back to Long Hái.

The following day, Williams and I brought a dozen of our strikers down to the beach to help us unload the boat. We mounted the engines, gassed her up and slid her into the water. The Cambodes couldn't believe their eyes. None of them had ever seen a boat like this, gleaming white with a midship steering wheel and a small windscreen. They swarmed it, jumping up and down like children. Williams took a few of them for a shake-down spin, then circled around to the beach and idled offshore.

"Hey McShane, you ready to ski?"

"Fuckin' A, man."

I grabbed the skis out of the truck, carried them into the water and put them on. One of the strikers handed me a life vest. Williams threw the ski rope handle toward me, and I waded out 'til water reached my belly. Leaning back, I squatted on the skis until I was floating in my vest, holding the rope handle between my legs. I was nervous. I hadn't skied since 1965, the summer before I enlisted. All I could think about was taking a spill and getting stung by a Portuguese Man O' War. I had already been stung by one swimming at the beach, and it hurt like a bastard.

"Hey, take up the slack," I shouted. Bill put the motors in gear and as the rope tightened, I thrust my right arm high in the air, my index finger pointing to the sky, and yelled "GO … GO … GO!"

The two engines roared to life, their power reaching down through my arms into my chest and torso, stretching, pulling, yanking my body out of the water, wind in my hair, the skis now surfing on the boat's wake. I was flying. The two Cambode spotters in the rear of the boat screamed, waving their arms at me in excitement, wondering at this marvel—Bác Sĩ standing on top of the water, chasing their boat, trying to catch them. Suddenly, I was skiing on Lake Ontario, my brother Matt and girlfriend Lisa in the boat pulling me around in giant circles, first the shoreline, then the horizon, and again and again. The sky was the brightest blue I could ever remember. The midafternoon sea breeze reminded me of trips to Cape Cod and Ocean City and Jones Beach. I was back home. Sea foam frothed over my feet, the warm, therapeutic saline mist soothed my body.

Williams signaled that he was heading in. I didn't want to stop. I could see the French hotel, a few people swimming in the surf, and the mountain beyond the village of Long Hái. And then, I was back to reality.

I took Williams skiing and after beaching the Whaler, grabbed a cooler full of cold Black Label out of the truck. We sat on the tailgate and tried to enjoy the rest of the afternoon. A few of the strikers wanted to ski, but none of them knew how to swim. Two weeks later, I scrounged a bunch of ski vests, and after teaching the strikers how to use them, we started with ski lessons. It was a howl.

The village of Long Hái was about five klicks down the road from Camp. There wasn't much to see: the main drag with a tailor shop, an auto-and-truck garage, a bicycle shop, and a cafe. It looked like a dusty Mexican border town. My first visit was just after getting back from the Devil's Triangle. Sgt. Donny Glenn, the senior medic whose tour would soon end, offered to show me around. It was the first time in country that I wore civvies: a blue, short-sleeve oxford shirt and cutoff Levis, a gift scented by the girl I had spent two weeks with while vacationing with my friend Tuna in Arizona before leaving for Nam. We parked the jeep in front of the cafe and walked into the veranda, where there were a half dozen tables with red-checked table cloths a la French country chic. Nice touch except for road dust and the pervasive stench of urine. It was about 1400 hours.

We sat down at a table in the corner adjacent to the front of the building and the short veranda wall. There was no one sitting behind us. A window opening next to the table gave us a full view of the interior of the cafe. There were a few men sitting together at one of the tables inside, and two guys sitting at one of the tables outside, at the other end of the veranda.

"The VC are thick in the hills, and it's a sure bet that any young men you see in town this time of day are VC."

"Jesus Christ, Donny. Why didn't we bring our weapons; at least a pistol?"

"You know the rule. It took me a while to get comfortable coming down here without a weapon."

"Then why are we here?"

"It's a game of balance. We leave them alone for the most part, and they leave us alone. I come in to do MEDCAP visits, and most of the patients I see are the families of these VC. They know we're medics and we help them."

I could feel my heart pumping. My hands turned cold.

"Man, I'm crawling in my underwear."

"Relax. See those guys inside?"

"Yeah."

"They're unarmed."

"Okay, so what?"

"They're probably on R&R or a day-pass. They aren't looking for trouble. Neither should we."

The waitress came and we ordered two Cokes. She asked if we wanted glasses with ice. Donny shook his head.

"Never drink the water, use ice or drink anything that isn't in a can or a bottle, got it?"

"What about the food?"

"Eat it cooked. You don't want dysentery. It'll knock the shit out of you, literally; same-same Mexico."

"Got it."

"Never go into town alone or in uniform. If you need something, send Trấn, our Vietnamese medic counterpart, down to get it. We get our Mike Force scarves from the tailor across the street. He's good. I did MEDCAP here once a month last year until Backus and Smyth got greased in August. Now we're short staffed, and in two weeks, you'll be all alone. Forget the MEDCAP until you get some reinforcements. Don't be a hero."

While Glenn was talking, I glanced at the guys at the table inside and they were all watching me. They looked like nondescript Vietnamese men, probably my age, but it freaked me out. I didn't know how I'd ever get comfortable with this program.

On the way back, we approached a French hotel, which was about a half-klick from Camp.

"You been here yet?"

I shook my head.

"Let's stop in. It's a nice place."

We pulled in off the road into a sand-covered parking area. The hotel was a pink stucco building on the beach, two stories, with a courtyard in front and a huge veranda on the backside facing the South China Sea. The windows were framed with louvered shutters painted cream, and the roof was covered in terra cotta tiles. A short wall circled the compound that was probably an acre in size.

The cultivated flower garden and mature trees looked out of place. The hotel had probably been there for close to a hundred years. Bougainvillea was planted along the wall and as we walked through the gate, their scent overcame me. Outside the compound were scrub bushes and sea grass. A large mahogany front door opened through a narrow vestibule to a small reception area with rattan furniture and a ceiling fan. We took a seat at a small mahogany bar with half a dozen rattan bar stools. The Vietnamese barkeep said: "Ba Mu'o'i Ba?"

"Ba Mu'o'i Ba tastes like shit. They have Black Label."

Donny ordered two and they were delivered almost instantaneously. We toasted.

"To a successful tour, my friend."

The beer was ice cold, dripping wet from an ice chest behind the bar. I took a couple of big gulps, the carbonation stinging my throat. My teeth ached momentarily, but it tasted so good. While we had beer at Camp, there is something to be said about ambiance, and this place had it. We took our drinks and walked down a long hall that ended at two French doors that opened onto the veranda. There were a few glass-topped tables, rattan chairs, and several rattan lounges. The view onto the beach was spectacular. It was about 1700 hours, and the sun was heavy in the western sky. There wasn't a cloud in sight, the horizon hazy with the humidity of the day. Several people swam in the surf. If it wasn't for the pervasive smell of burning brush, inescapable in Vietnam, I'd have thought it was Nassau.

"What do you think?" asked Glenn.

"I'm impressed."

"The Europeans have it right. Drive down here for a long weekend. Eat some native shrimp, catch a few rays. It's a lot cooler here than in Saigon."

After spending almost two years in training being told that this was a war zone, I'm relaxing at a resort. Are these people stupid, or am I just gullible, a dumb GI? What am I missing?

"This whole scene blows me away. There's a war going on across the road and people over here frolic in the surf, drink champagne, and eat shrimp."

"Believe it, man. The rest of the world carries on while we lead the charge against communism, the imminent threat that it is to us." Glen glanced at me while shaking his head.

"My recommendation—make the best of it while you're here."

Dispensary

The pregnant woman collapsed at the triage station, sprawling over the desk, sending its contents crashing to the floor. Her arms reached to embrace the startled nurse, seizing an amulet of the Buddha hanging from a chain around the nurse's neck.

"Bác Sĩ … Bác Sĩ!"

Her muffled cries were barely intelligible over the screams of protest from a toddler I was wrestling in the back of the dispensary. He had a splinter the size of a pencil jammed under his toenail and wasn't about to let me touch his toe, which was swollen and stunk with infection. His hysterical mother wasn't much help, either.

That morning, the tiny dispensary, a beach cottage on the shores of the South China Sea, seemed even smaller than usual with the din of sick call; it was pandemonium. The room was packed with patients from our mercenary encampment across the road, triaged and waiting. When I was in camp, the indigenous medics and nurses deferred to me. Breathe. I wanted nothing more than to join the European vacationers down the beach at the French hotel. Their children frolicked in the surf while they relaxed on the veranda, gorging themselves on shrimp and sipping champagne. The acrid early morning air, heavy with the scent of burning brush from a thousand cooking fires, was a ready reminder that life on this beach was anything but a day at the beach.

"Bác Sĩ … Bác Sĩ!"

I handed the boy off to a nurse and ran up to the triage station where the young woman had collapsed and fallen to the plywood floor. Sand swirled around her body like she was sea grass. One of the indigenous medics and I carefully lifted her flaccid form onto a stretcher, hands still clutching the nurse's Buddha in a death-grip.

"Loan, take her to one of the tables in the back."

Loan, a nurse, had no formal training. A Cambodian woman, about 30 years old, she was good with patients, but spoke little English. Her vocabulary was limited to dispensary-talk, like "take her to the table," "take her blood pressure," or "give her a 5cc injection of penicillin."

The patient was probably not more than 14, small in stature with high cheekbones, raven hair, and supple bronze skin. She looked like so many of the vacationers' children seen romping on the beach across the road. But she was a Cambode, and females in peasant families were married off early.

Pupils dilated. Breathing labored. Fever of 104. Blood pressure of 94/60. I palpated her abdomen. It was distended and taut beyond pregnancy. I passed smelling salts under her nose with no effect. Her airway was clear but she had a weak pulse. Dehydration. Or worse. She was alone. Her husband was probably out on one of our search-and-destroy missions, gone for a week or two.

"Trấn, get me a liter of Ringers lactate and a setup. We need to get some fluid into her."

He was my senior medic, a middle-aged Vietnamese man who had trained with the French in the early 50s, and after Dien Bien Phou, went to work at a hospital in Vũng Tàu. When the US started sending Special Forces A-Teams into country in the early '60s, he came to work for us. Trấn was only proficient to a point, but spoke English well.

I looked at her lying on the table and thought about possible ailments. I knew she was dehydrated, but that could have been caused by any number of things. Dehydration and diarrhea were rampant in country. An hour on a fast drip IV and she would show signs of improvement. Could she have an ectopic pregnancy? God, I hoped not. We couldn't treat her here. Resources weren't available for anything more exotic than common ailments, cuts and bruises; sepsis was a joke. In a pinch, we did minor surgery, but serious cases were referred up to the Special Forces C-Team in Bien Hoa or to one of the regional Vietnamese hospitals.

"Trấn, what do you think?"

"Bác Sĩ, I think she has a complication with her pregnancy."

"Why do you say that?"

"She has come to the dispensary before. Last week she complained of lightheadedness and tenderness in her belly."

"What did you do for her?"

"I told her to go to bed and stay off her feet."

"Trấn, why didn't you tell me that before?"

"Bác Sĩ, I was helping another patient and forgot. She was here last week when you were out on a mission."

Why should I be surprised? I spent most of my time on missions. None of my teammates wanted to go in the field without a medic. Since I was the only one left, I went. I didn't chew out Trấn because he hadn't diagnosed the problem last week when we might have had time to get a consultation from the doctor at the C-Team. Sick call went on, whether or not I was in camp.

Trấn's comments confirmed my diagnosis. She needed to go to a hospital, but Cambodians were at the bottom of the ethnic ladder in Vietnam and she might not receive treatment. It was the only option to save her life.

"Trấn, can you find someone in the village who can take her to the Vũng Tàu hospital?"

Top wouldn't let me use one of our Jeeps. I'd already wrecked one the week before on a similar mission racing to the hospital at Vũng Tàu. He didn't want me risking my life on the highway, which was often mined.

"Bác Sĩ, isn't there anything we can do?"

I wanted to call in a chopper and whisk her to the MASH in Bien Hoa, but there was no way that Top would authorize it. Our Cambodian mercenaries, and by extension their families, were expendable.

"We can't treat her here, Trấn. She needs surgery ASAP or she'll die."

Trấn worked his network of contacts in the village and soon an old man with a tiny three-wheel Lambretta truck pulled up to the dispensary, backing up to the door. We gathered up the young woman on a stretcher and carefully placed her in the bed of the truck. It didn't fit well, her feet sticking out beyond the bumper, but it was the best we could do.

The little truck bobbed and struggled through the beach sand on its way to the highway at the edge of camp, its cargo bouncing around like a load of lumber. Weekenders from Saigon and Vũng Tàu clogged the highway with their ancient Peugeots and Renaults. They cruised among military vehicles, on the way to resorts along the South China seacoast. I knew it would take at least two hours to go to Vũng Tàu with all the traffic, assuming that the old man wasn't forced off the road by an army deuce-and-a-half. Crushing Lambros was considered a sport by some GIs. Anyway, I guessed she'd be dead by then. Top didn't want anyone dying in our dispensary. He said it was bad for mercenary morale.

Katum

There wasn't much said about Cambodia during training, so I didn't know what to expect, other than the fact that we weren't supposed to be there. Everybody was shooting the shit before dinner, and the subject of Cambodia came up. Jones, the Camp commander, said that he had run several recon patrols out to the border, about eight klicks away, and that there was plenty of enemy activity. Prince Sihanouk, while publicly taking a neutral stance on the war, was thought to sympathize with the North Vietnamese, and allowed them to use Cambodia as a staging area for their operations into South Vietnam. In fact, Jones said that the Ho Chi Minh Trail, which ran from Hanoi through Cambodia and ended in Sihanoukville on the South China Sea, was just over the border. The trail was the main supply route for the North's war effort. Special Forces was interdicting the trail as it ran through Laos, but the enemy had a free run in Cambodia.

The Mike Force had been running operations deep into Cambodia for over two years, with some degree of success. Teams didn't have to go very far over the border to find what they were looking for. The NVA had upward of 20 base camps along the Trail, where units could regroup, train, and prepare for operations in the south. There were training camps for local VC and stockpiles of food, ammunition, clothing, and equipment. The Trail consisted of roads, trails, and footpaths, depending on the terrain. The enemy ran at night, under the cover of darkness. I couldn't help myself and asked Bill what it was like.

"There's a fucking gravelled highway two lanes wide just over the border from here. You can hear tanks and trucks running it at night. It's scary, man. God help you if you run into shit that you can't handle. There's no air support and no medevacs. It's restricted airspace, and because of that, the enemy has free run of the place. We've been real careful, but we've always made contact. We hit and run, but there is no way that a company-sized operation could hold off an NVA battalion or regiment. So we just harass the shit out of them and run back across the border, hoping that they follow us. When they do, we bring in the heavy guns and air support and kick their ass. It's fucking great."

As Williams talked, I remembered training for clandestine operations in Uwharrie, but those were war games. Now, there was an enemy. This was the real thing.

THE DRONE OF THE GENERATOR was the only sound I could hear that evening. The camp was lit up like the boardwalk at Coney Island. Floodlights illuminated the compound inside the berm, so if the camp was attacked at night, we could see the enemy. Nighttime belonged to Victor Charlie. I laid out a bedroll on a stretcher I found in one of the sandbagged Conex containers. The smell of canvas warm from the humid heat of the day burned my nostrils. It was pitch black save for a shard of blue-white light shining through a crack in the sandbag wall, lighting up my corner of the container. As I rested my head on the soft side of my field rig, I watched as millions of specks of dust danced on the beam of light, changing hue but not intensity. I felt like one of those specks floating through space. What was I doing in Southeast Asia?

Stevens came in to wake me up the next morning. I hadn't slept well. I woke up every time I turned over in my bedroll, the stretcher not giving me any respite. The noise of the generator didn't help either. It was 0510 and chow was in 20 minutes. I had to get my gear together and bring it over to the team house by 0530. The sun was bright on the horizon, shining through portals in the sandbag walls and illuminating the container. I rolled over on my side to see what the room looked like in daylight. It was about seven feet high, the same wide and 12 feet long, with a half dozen stretchers strewn about, stored there by the camp medic. I suppose a stretcher beat sleeping on the metal floor. As I looked at the thick sandbag walls inside the steel box, I felt a sense of security, and yet concern, because the room could easily morph into a tomb under incoming artillery. We were close enough to the NVA encampments in Cambodia to have to worry about that. I rolled off the stretcher and struggled to my feet, body aching. I grabbed my field harness and M-16, and stepped out into the daylight, squinting. Days seemed to start instantly in Vietnam. Once the sun rose over the horizon, it was bright daylight.

After chow, I grabbed LRRPs for five days, filled a canteen with water, and then went over to the ammo dump to pick up two grenades, two smoke bombs, and eight loaded twenty-round magazines for the M-16. I taped the magazines back to back and stowed everything in my field rig.

Stevens and I went over to where the strikers were staged to make sure that they were ready to move out. Our mercenary companies were organized in much the same way as an army infantry company. There was a company commander, an executive officer, and six platoons: one recon, three rifle and two weapons, a combination of M-60 machine guns and M-79 grenade launchers. Americans led the companies as CO and XO, Stevens and me in this case, and an ARVN Special Forces advisor provided indigenous leadership. The platoon leaders and squad leaders were Cambodian.

The four companies gathered outside the berm adjacent to the airstrip. We had a last-minute debriefing to review the mission plan and then we were off at 0600. We quickly crossed the airstrip to gain the cover of the jungle and headed for the end of the runway where we would enter the jungle on a bearing of 270 degrees. We split up into two columns spread 50 meters apart, with the recon platoon running about a hundred meters ahead of both columns. Stevens was in the recon platoon and I was in one of the columns with Williams. Son Trẻ, my Cambodian medic, was with me. Kim Trung, an ARVN Special Forces advisor, was with the other column. Each column and the recon platoon had a Cambode radioman. Our objective for the day was to cover the eight klicks between the camp and the border looking for signs of enemy activity, either VC or NVA regulars. VC trainees from the NVA training camps in Cambodia cut their teeth harassing our A-Camps.

The jungle in this part of the country was much like the forests of North Carolina where we trained, but much thicker with lush vegetation and undergrowth that made it difficult to walk. Except for the sounds of our feet crushing vegetation, the jungle was silent, which added to the suspense; it was foreboding. Tropical trees a hundred feet tall and plants with leaves as large as a man's body made me feel like an insect in a trap. Vines went on endlessly, some as thick as a man's arm. It was the dry season, which made traveling easier, but you still needed a machete to make any headway. The canopy was so thick that it blocked out the sun, making it feel like twilight. It also didn't do much to cool the air. By midmorning, temperatures in Vietnam this time of year were in the 90s, climbing to over 100 degrees by midafternoon. It was so humid that perspiration was inevitable even if you weren't exerting yourself.

That made walking through the jungle a real effort. Visibility was often less than 10 meters.

It was difficult communicating with the indigenous troops on operations because you couldn't see them, and the language barrier made it even more frustrating. Thankfully, we had a handful of colloquialisms that covered 80 percent of communication needs, with the rest covered by pantomime. If you were lucky, there were a few that knew enough English that you didn't need a translator, but in the heat of battle, you hoped that pointing, shouting, and gesturing got the message across.

When moving from one locale to another, we always opted for travel under cover, rather than in the open through farmers' fields and rice paddies, where our whereabouts would be obvious. Sometimes I wondered whether we were any safer in the jungle, since Charlie was there.

A few minutes later, Steven's voice crackled over the PRC-25 telling us to move out. The plan was to continue hiking until 1300 and break for chow. The jungle was getting thicker and more difficult to penetrate. Visibility worsened. A half hour into the hike, one of my Cambodes at the front of the column ran back to tell me that they had found the remnants of cooking fires. I called Stevens and Trung to let them know that we were stopping to reconnoiter the situation. Williams and I walked up to the head of the column and sure enough, there were hot coals left from three recent fires. They must have reconned our movement that morning and high-tailed it out. I called Stevens to let him know and just then AK-47 rifle fire broke out ahead of us.

"China Boy 32 Zulu, this is China Boy 32 Alpha, over."

"Go ahead, Steve."

"We've got what appears to be a platoon-size element ahead of us. Flank me on my left and I'll tell Trung to do the same on my right, over."

I could feel my heart race as our column ran forward the hundred meters to flank Stevens's platoon. As we got into position, rifle fire exploded. I hit the ground behind a giant tree root just in time, because the bark on the tree began popping off in shards. Now some of the Cambodes in front of me were returning fire. I couldn't see them, but I could tell by the sound of their weapons, all of which have distinctive voices. Our Cambodes had M-2 carbines; the enemy had AK-47s; and the Americans had CAR-15s or M-16s. I looked to either side of my position and could see three Cambodes spread out to my left; Williams and two Cambodes were to my right; I had the radioman and Son Trẻ with me. None of us were shooting because of the dense underbrush. We knew there were Cambodes in front of us.

"China Boy 32 Alpha, this is China Boy 32 Zulu, over."

"Come in, Pete."

"What's going on up there, Jim?"

Stevens said that he thought he had underestimated the size of the enemy force, and it might be a company-size element. He told me to make sure that my column was lined up 210 degrees/30 degrees, and to take cover because he was calling in artillery. We had about three minutes before the shit would hit the fan. Because visibility was so poor, we never knew whether the Cambodes were where they were supposed to be. They were merciless, more like a band of hooligans rather than trained warriors.

"Hold on to your jock strap, out."

The incoming artillery sounded like rockets coming in over our heads and felt close enough to reach up and touch: the whistle, whoosh, a second or two of silence and then an overwhelming ka-boom and aftershock. The ground shuddered; dirt and debris flew everywhere. The explosions were deafening; my ears would ring for hours, sometimes days after the blasts. I felt alternating waves of fear and comfort as the rounds came in and delivered their devastating blows. We were fortunate to be within range of the Camp's battery of 105mm Howitzers. They weren't the biggest artillery piece in country, but they were all we had and they were accurate as hell; you could bring them into a target a square meter in size. I never thought I'd welcome the smoke, the choking, acrid smell of nitrates.

The first five rounds came in about 50 meters out. Then Stevens walked them out another 20 meters, under the assumption that the enemy might be running for it. A simple mistake on map coordinates, a fraction of a klick, is all it would take to turn us into mincemeat. After the last round detonated, there was an eerie silence, just dust and clouds of acrid blue smoke, cordite that burned the throat and nostrils with every breath.

"China Boy 32 Zulu, this is China Boy 32 Alpha, over."

"Go ahead, Jim."

"You okay over there?"

"Roger, just can't hear."

"You'll get over it. Check out your column for casualties and then take one of your platoons and check out the enemy's position, over."

Things happened so fast that there wasn't time to assess casualties during the firefight. Word came back through the column that there were two wounded Cambodes. These would be my first two since arriving in Vietnam. As Son Trẻ and I went out to the end of the column, all I could think about was whether I'd be able to help them. I had the training, but this was the real thing. We found a squad leader with a superficial leg wound and one of his men with an abdominal wound. The squad leader's leg wasn't bleeding, so I told Son Trẻ to clean him up and apply a field dressing, while I looked at the guy with the gut wound. The entry wound was a small, tight hole right over the spleen, I rolled him over and the exit wound was the size of a golf ball. I couldn't tell if the spleen or kidney had been hit, but chances were good it was one or both of them. He was bleeding from the exit wound and the ground underneath him was saturated with blood. He needed surgery ASAP if he had any chance of surviving. A liter of Ringers lactate IV would help to stabilize him, but only temporarily. We didn't medevac indigenous troops, nor did we carry IV solutions for them; our strikers were considered expendable, according to Top. I carried lifesaving supplies for the Americans, and they were the only ones that we medevaced. Under the circumstances, this guy was going to die while we were on our mission. I told Son Trê to make him as comfortable as possible, and to gather a few of the men to make stretchers for the two soldiers. We carried our dead and wounded with us.

I felt pretty good about how I reacted to the casualties, but I wasn't mentally prepared for the decision to withhold care to the man who needed an IV and surgery. The subject didn't come up in training per se, but neither did the subject of limited resources. This scene would play out again in future firefights. I'd bend the rules whenever I could, but I didn't like playing the role of God. I felt guilty for not having done more for our strikers. I wasn't the guy in charge, but it didn't make me feel any better.

Williams and I rounded up the first platoon and we spread out single file to comb the area in front of our position. Bomb craters smoldered. The kill zone was littered with diabolical shapes and heaps of ash; bodies mangled, deformed, and lifeless. The smell of burning flesh is like none other. Its slimy metallic taste lingers in the mouth for days. There was blood everywhere, as if someone had dropped a grenade into a drum of it; it covered the trees and leaves and left puddles on the jungle floor. There were chunks of flesh hanging from tree branches. My stomach was in knots, unstrung by the human devastation. They never trained us for this.

Errant shots could be heard as we walked, and I hit the turf, concerned that it was enemy fire. Williams walked over nonchalantly and said that it was the Cambodes finishing off the enemy wounded.

"You've got to be kidding?"

"No, Bro. These guys mean business."

"What about prisoners; don't we interrogate them?"

"We do if the Cambodes don't get to them first."

"Why don't we do something about it, Bill?"

"Listen. These guys are the KKK."

"So what?"

"Khmer Kampuchea Krom. They hate the Vietnamese. They've been persecuted by them for over 200 years. Did you know that they were in Vietnam long before the Vietnamese got here?"

"No," I said, incredulous.

"The KKK hate communists, and are fighting for us as a way to crush Sihanouk's government. They want to take back their government, and they want us to go with them."

"You've got to be shitting me."

"One of these days, we'll be going into Cambodia supporting them, mark my words."

Just then, one of my Cambode squad leaders came running through the jungle with the rest of his squad following closely behind, cheering and cajoling one another. As he approached, I could see that he was carrying something. From a distance, it looked like a sack of rice or a live hen, but when he came into focus, it was an NVA soldier's head freshly relieved of his body. The Cambode came up to me directly, raising the head up for me to see. The dead soldier was a boy, maybe 15. His eyes were open and black as night, his mouth shaped as if he were in midsentence pleading, "Stop, please stop." The process of decapitating him must have taken some effort, because his neck had been hacked multiple times with a machete, leaving a jagged edge of muscle and sinew. There were three or four segments of the spine hanging below the neck muscles, as well as a length of the esophagus, which looked like a section of armored electrical cable, the segments glistening in blood. The carotid arteries and jugulars dangled like wires from an old light fixture. Blood sprayed on me as the Cambode swung the head around for everyone to see. My stomach cramped and I could feel its contents rushing toward my mouth. I had everything I could do to keep my composure.

"Son Trẻ, tell him to take the head away and put it with the corpse."

Williams could see that I was deeply shaken, and he came over and put his hand on my shoulder.

"Why the fuck do we put up with this brutality?"

"I know that this is difficult to understand, because we come from the civilized world where there is the rule of law. These Cambodes are fighting for their lives; we're just along for the ride."

"What happened to the Geneva Convention?" I said.

"There is no Geneva Convention out here. It's kill or be killed, pure and simple."

I came across one enemy soldier cowering in a shallow depression. He had a scalp laceration and burns on his arms, but otherwise he was okay, just scared shitless. He got up on his knees and put his hands together as if praying to me. He had the uniform of an NVA regular on, but he couldn't have been more than 16 or 17. He was jabbering in Vietnamese.

"What is he saying?"

"Bác Sĩ, he is pleading not to kill him. He has an elderly mother and a sister that need his support. His father was killed by the French at Dien Bien Phou, and his older brother was killed last year by us in Laos."

"Tell him that I'm not going to kill him, but he has to cooperate with us."

I could see the soldier nod his head as Son Trẻ spoke to him.

I lifted the soldier up on his feet and looked over his head wound.

"Get me some 4×4s and a canteen of water."

As I cleaned up his scalp, I decided the laceration wasn't deep enough to suture, so I put a field bandage on his head and wrapped it with a length of white cloth. This was a way for us to keep track of prisoners. Son Trẻ cleaned up the burns on his arms, applied salve and wrapped them in gauze. This was as good as it was going to get under field conditions. I worried that he'd become a casualty before the operation was over, and within two hours I heard gunshots. The Cambodes had killed him despite my objections.

AT THE END OF THE DAY we struck camp between the Ho Chi Minh Trail and the Cambodian border. Cambodes had killed another four NVA, and, of course, there were no prisoners. I felt like I had done something wrong by saving that kid's life. Later, Stevens told me not to waste my time treating wounded enemy. I was conflicted over the logic of military orders and the casual way that my teammates interpreted it. It flew in the face of everything I had ever been taught growing up—the sanctity of life; treating others as you would like to be treated. Maybe it was the only way that they could deal with the brutality and chaos of war: to make light of it. I knew war would be bad, but the way we practiced it in war games was not realistic.

That night, as I lay in my hammock in the darkness of the dense vegetation, we were less than 300 meters from the Trail. I could hear the traffic, the sound of trucks and tanks rumbling through the jungle. It was frightening. I don't think I ever felt so alone in my life.

Grand Hotel

Vũng Tàu was a party town. There were over a hundred bars, many of them named after American cities, an obvious attempt to attract the thousands of GIs roaming the streets. Not only did Americans and Aussies use Vũng Tàu as an in-country R&R center, but so did the VC. After my introduction to this phenomenon in Long Hái, I got used to the idea of sharing the country with the enemy.

On an overnight, I'd check in at the Grand Hotel. It was an elegant leftover from the French Colonial era, with whitewashed exterior, shuttered arched windows and a terra cotta tile roof. A giant neon sign, no doubt added for the benefit of GIs, stood prominently over the entrance, announcing that it was air-conditioned. The hotel compound was situated across the street from Front Beach, a beautiful stretch of white sand. It was the only hotel in the city that had a comfortable pub off the lobby that served food. The formal dining room overlooking the courtyard and trellised patio served full meals. The food was almost as good as that of Lee Chang, our Chinese chef. Patrons dressed for dinner, often in eveningwear. In the morning, my favorite meal was the chef's special mushroom omelet with Muenster and a cup of French Roast coffee.

The hotel had been a headquarters for French soldiers during the colonial period. Many American and Australian officers now had permanent quarters at the Grand. It was charming, and close to an experience I might have had in Hawaii or Miami. The only thing I couldn't get legally at hotels back home was female companionship, and the Grand came through in style. Attached to the hotel compound was an annex occupied by 80 gái mai dâm—prostitutes. The Grand was a bordello in the French tradition. The mamasan was a stunning, middle-aged, French Vietnamese woman who ruled her brood in no uncertain terms. You could have any variety of woman you wanted: tall, short, slender, buxom, and almost any nationality: Vietnamese, French, Cambodian, Chinese, Laotian. It was a candy store. That's how we thought of it back then, a treat to look forward to after the mind-numbing fear of firefights. Instead of names, the women had numbers ranging from one to 80, easy to remember after an afternoon of drinking. One to 10 were in training, and you could only buy them Saigon Tea—no boom-boom. From 11 to 80 it was open season: one-on-one boom-boom, *ménage à trois*, or whatever suited you at the moment. Gái mai dâm were registered with the government, tested for venereal diseases, and required to carry yellow ID cards. There were strict rules enforced by the mamasan: the two of you showered before and after having sex; you wore a condom, and no brutality was allowed—fair enough.

A typical overnight followed a weeklong field operation. We'd be completely spent emotionally and physically. Arriving at the hotel midday, we'd start drinking the poison; my drug of choice was JB and Coke. There'd be a half dozen of us racing to the finish. Those of us who had paced ourselves–not many, would have some food. If we were still functioning, we'd check out mamasan's inventory sitting at the bar or in one of the lounge chairs. If none of the women present suited us, or we had a favorite, we'd pay a visit to Mama. She'd patiently listen to us trying to speak coherently, and give us a choice of the women who were in her suite. You didn't want to get into an argument with her. I did one night, over a woman who decided that I was too drunk to perform. She was right, of course, but that didn't matter; it was the principle of the thing. I had already paid. Mama reluctantly refunded my money, but told me never to come back. Of course, a few weeks later, money talked.

The Grand Hotel helped us forget the awful shit that went on in the field. I was able to go back to Camp and face another operation, hoping that I'd be alive for another trip to town.

One evening there was a group of our Mike Force guys and six or seven from B-36 Mobile Guerilla all sitting in the pub getting oiled. We were talking shop, chest pounding about the last operation, the bullet or shrapnel wounds endured, or the VC someone had taken down with a club. I was blind drunk, and in the mood for frivolity. I stumbled over to the bar to talk with one of the women I knew and asked if I could borrow her nightie for a half hour. She had no idea what I wanted, but I remembered that many of the women spoke French. When I said negligee and pointed to myself, she looked confused. "For me," I said. She frowned, shook her head, but rose from her chair and took me by the hand up to her room. I stripped down to my skivvies and put on her negligee; she burst into laughter! "You crazy, GI!" I walked down the large, center aisle staircase to the lobby in my baby-dolls. The gái mai dâm in the pub screeched in laughter. I flitted around the lobby shaking my booty for all the GIs. The guys erupted in gut-wrenching laughter. The reactions of a few staid officers in the lobby nursing their afternoon tea were priceless. One of them almost fell out of his chair with laughter. Another suggested that I was out of line. I thought that he had said I was out of uniform, so I told him I was on holiday.

There was a dark side to our trips to Vũng Tàu. Get to drinking and the emotions that had been bottled up for days would explode, coming out of nowhere. The streets could be dangerous. Gangs of young Vietnamese toughs would take advantage of drunks, roll them, strip them of their wallets and leave them for dead. Then there were the GIs. With somewhere near 25,000 stationed at bases there, plus guys on in-country R&R, you knew that shit would happen. The MPs roamed the streets to keep the peace, but anything was possible when soldiers drank.

Strout, Hudson, and Hopkins, all lifers, came in with me one Saturday afternoon after a weeklong operation at Katum, most of it over the border in Cambodia. Williams had gotten wounded. We were spent. We parked the jeep in a back lot of the hotel and had a beer in the pub. Strout, an average-size guy, but muscular, was talking about some Leg he had gotten into a fight with two weeks earlier at a bar called Lucky 7, down at the other end of Front Beach. The guy had seen Stevens's beret and called him a pussy. Strout had all but beaten the man senseless, when some of the guy's buddies jumped in and pulled Strout off. In the process, they kicked the shit out of him and broke a couple of ribs. I had taped him up back at camp. Strout was a level-headed guy, a black belt in Goju-Ryu, and always seemed to be in control, that is until he got drunk, which was pretty much every time he drank beer. He wanted us to go with him back to Lucky 7.

"Hey, man, you're crazier than I thought," said Hudson, our demolition sergeant. He was fortyish, heavy-set, and had a dry sense of humor. "Why would you want to ruin a perfectly good evening of drinking and fucking by getting into a fight with some Leg asshole—don't get enough excitement in the field?"

Strout shook his head.

"That's not it, man. You don't get it."

"Oh, I get it. Your feelings were hurt. 'No Leg is going to embarrass me'."

Hudson hit a chord. Strout was staring at the bottles on the bar back.

"Okay, I admit it, but it was my fault. I was too drunk to defend myself. If I had been sober, I could have kicked the shit out of all of them."

"But you weren't," said Hudson, taking a sip of beer.

I could feel tension build. I had no interest in a bar fight.

"Hey, Bill, why don't you just cool it here," said Hopkins, our intel sergeant. He was a pay grade higher than all of us.

"You guys hungry?" I said. "I can taste the Grand burger and fries."

I glanced at my three compadres waiting for approval.

"Doc, the voice of sense," said Hudson. "Let's grab our booth and get down to business."

Our booth, what we called the "Communal Tribunal," took up a whole corner in the pub. It was a large semicircle of rolled and pleated leather, about 15 feet in diameter. It could seat a dozen of us. We'd critique our operations, tell stories, and otherwise entertain one another and the rest of the room after a few drinks.

A waiter came over to the table. We ordered food and another round of drinks. Meanwhile, some guys from B-36 joined us. On weekends, there was always a group at the table. Guys would come and go.

It was almost 1700 when we finished our meals. Hudson leaned over, toothpick stuck in the corner of his mouth: "I think it's time to get down to business. What do you think?"

I was drinking JB and Coke and feeling no pain.

"Sure, lead the way."

THE NEXT MORNING, I was down in the lobby at around 0530 getting a cup of French Roast from the maître d', when I saw Strout sneaking into the lobby like he was on a mission. His fatigues were damp and covered in sand.

"Where you been, passed out on Front Beach?"

"Fuck. We've got to get out of here. Go get Hudson and I'll get Hopkins. The MPs are after me."

I rushed up to the room and woke Hudson. He wasn't happy.

"Strout, the party prevention department."

We gathered our gear, checked out, and went to our jeep parked behind the hotel. Not a minute later, Strout and Hopkins showed up. We headed out of town as fast as we could. Strout was behind the wheel, and the traffic on a Sunday morning was heavy. The local markets were open and people were milling around the street, buying fruits, vegetables, fish, and chicken. I never could imagine eating any of the meat or fish at those markets, which had been out in the heat all day and covered with flies. Traffic was crawling.

"God damn it. Get these fuckers out of the way."

Strout was possessed, and kept looking over his shoulder.

"What the fuck is going on?" said Hudson.

"I got into it last night. I found that asshole."

"Do you have a fucking death wish?"

"I guess I do. We went out in the street, and his buds followed him. Things started to go around in my head. I pulled out my 38 and started firing into the air. I don't know why. The guys scattered, leaving me alone in the middle of the street. Then I heard sirens, and knew the MPs were on their way."

He had ducked into an alley behind the bar and made his way to the beach where he hid until daybreak.

"That Leg might have remembered my name."

By this time, we had reached the intersection of Route 2, about half way to Long Hái. There was a cafe at the corner just before the turn, and we hadn't had any breakfast.

"Stop here," said Hudson.

Strout looked at him, fear in his eyes.

“You’re safe with us, man. We just came from camp to have some lunch. Got it? Don’t fucking worry about it.”

We grabbed a table toward the rear of the restaurant so as to watch the entry door.

“Did you shoot anybody?” asked Hopkins.

“I don’t know. I don’t think so … can’t remember.”

Strout had the DTs. He spilled water all over himself, and quickly stood up.

“I’m fucked up. God damn it. How do I get into this shit?”

Sitting back down, he shook his head back and forth as if scanning the room for an answer, slammed his fist on the table and burst into tears. We sat there watching him melt down. There wasn’t anything we could do.

Us younger guys would often laugh at the career guys, call them lifers, ridicule and cajole them, but on operations, they were the ones who kept us alive. All of us drank too much, so who was going to throw the first stone?

Minefield

Claymore mines and concertina wire lined the perimeter of our camp. The territory beyond that was littered with old mines, buried years before by the French. We cleared what we could when we built our camp, but there were still leftovers. Every so often, someone would wander off the road and trip one of them. We'd get the casualties at the dispensary. Most were DOA.

It was a day in early spring, hot and humid. The sun blazed and sand burned my feet as it crept into the crevices of my jungle boots. After a morning spent in the dispensary, I was on my way back from mess when Trấn ran up to me, out of breath and anxious.

"Bác Sĩ, there's a little boy from our camp wandering in the minefield across the road."

"How the hell did that happen? Where was his mother?"

"I don't know, Bác Sĩ. The child strayed off chasing a cat and ran into the minefield after it. His older brother just ran into the dispensary to tell me."

Trấn and I jumped into a jeep and raced out of the compound. About two klicks down the road, I could see a woman at the edge of a field of sea grass waving her arms, and a four-year-old boy standing in a patch of sand about a hundred meters off the road. She was frantic.

"Trấn, what is the woman saying?"

"Bác Sĩ, she is telling the boy to come back to the road."

"No … No … No! Trấn, tell her to make him stay where he is!"

All I could visualize was the boy running toward us, tripping one of those mines, his body atomizing in front of us. We jumped out of the jeep and ran over to the woman. She was shaking, sobbing uncontrollably.

Afraid for my life, I didn't know what to do: leave and hope that he didn't blow himself up, or go and get him? Hesitating a moment, I took another look at the child's desperate mother, and decided that I had to go after him.

"Trấn, tell her that I'm going to get the boy. Have her tell him to stay where he is: Do-Not-Move."

"Bác Sĩ, you shouldn't go into the minefield."

"What would you do, Trấn, wait for the boy to trip a mine and watch him blow up in our faces? It's too late to back out now. I have to do this."

I tried frantically to remember what I had learned in training classes. "Put your feet one in front of the other in measured steps, touching the ground first with the ball of your foot, lowering it to your heel, slowly shifting your weight to the ball of the other foot. Scan the ground in front of you for trip wires, or prongs. Look for things that appear to be growing out of the ground that look unnatural."

"Trấn, ask her the boy's name."

"Bác Sĩ, it is Loi."

Terrified, I began taking slow steps toward the child, praying that he would not become frightened and run from me, or worse, toward me. He was only a hundred meters away, but it seemed like a kilometer. I took one step after another, scanning the ground for signs of a mine. Visions of chunks of my body floating through space consumed my thoughts, but prongs sticking up just a meter in front of me brought me back to reality in a hurry. As long as I can see the wires or prongs, I'll be okay, I thought. The field was beach sand, with alternate windswept mounds held together with sea grass, and valleys of bare patches where you could see the mines plain as day. I stayed off of the mounds where prongs or trip wires might be buried. I figured that my chances were better in the valleys where I could at least see signs of the ordnance.

It must have taken me 20 minutes to reach the boy and all I could think about was him running and blowing us both to bits. He was just standing there, with a mischievous look, not sure why his mother was so upset. Thank God he recognized me from the dispensary and didn't try to run away.

"Loi … Bác Sĩ wants to take you to your mother. Stay there," I said in a calm voice, while my body shook under my tiger fatigues. Then he playfully turned away to goad me into a chase, and began to run toward the sea, about 300 meters away. I knew I only had one chance to grab him. I lunged and snagged the sleeve of his shirt. He fell backward toward me. I lost my footing and landed in the sand on top of him. For a few seconds there was silence. Then he burst into giggles.

"Bác Sĩ … more, more!"

I lay there trembling, clutching the little boy in my arms and fighting back my tears. Scanning the ground, I saw a trip wire sticking out of the sand just an arm's length away from us. I hugged the boy as hard as I could, and as I did, he began laughing, tears of pleasure running down his face. My body was wracked with the pain of fear, but his joy soothed me. Get control of yourself, I thought. You still have to make it back to the road. I told Loi that we would play again once we got back to the road. With the boy in my arms, I started to backtrack, trying desperately to concentrate on what I had to do.

I don't remember much about the return trip. Somehow we made it back and I delivered the little boy into his mother's arms. I was exhausted and relieved.

That afternoon, Trần, Loan, and I took a jeep across the road to the encampment to hold a MEDCAP. We tried to do this once a week when I was in camp. Sometimes the strikers were too sick to come to the dispensary. Other times, they didn't want to bother us, mostly out of ignorance. Most of them had never been seen by a doctor before signing on as our mercenaries. It was easier for them if we went there, sort of like making house calls. We'd walk the aisles of their hooches, all joined together in a common hallway, and look in on their lives. This day was different. When our jeep approached the entryway to the compound, we were swarmed by hundreds of people.

"Bác Sĩ … Bac, Si … Bác Sĩ!"

The crowd was yelling at us. I was concerned for our safety. They didn't seem angry, but they were agitated for some reason.

"What's going on Trần; what are they saying?"

"Bác Sĩ, they're praising you; they're thanking you for saving that little boy."

From the back of the crowd came Noh, a Cambodian elder and the self-appointed mayor of the encampment. He walked up to my side of the jeep and grabbed my arm.

"Bác Sĩ, we are happy that you saved Loi," he said in broken English. "You faced great danger to save him and we are happy for you."

I didn't know what to say. Women and men swarmed the jeep, touching me and bowing. Noh reached into the pocket of his jacket and pulled out a folded white cloth and a small gold and ivory Buddha amulet on a chain. Almost every one of our strikers had one of these icons hanging around his neck. Superstition or not, they felt safe in the Buddha's presence. He took the white cloth and opened it up to reveal a prayer cloth, a half-meter square made out of linen. It was hand-printed with an intricate array of icons and prayers in Khmer. I remember seeing our mercenaries carry them.

"Bác Sĩ, you carry this prayer cloth and the Buddha with you. It protect you from harm."

I thought about how the Cambodes put those amulets in their mouths during firefights, and wondered if there was anything to it.

When Top found out about my foray into the minefield, he was livid, his face flush and eyes on fire.

"McShane, what the fuck were you thinking, going out into a minefield to rescue a gook kid?

"Top, I just did my job."

"McShane, your job is to protect the Americans, not risk your life saving some Cambodian kid."

"But they're our mercenaries; they're family. I did what I thought was right."

"They aren't your family; they're not our family. You risked your life needlessly. It's hard enough staying alive on our operations. You don't need to risk it here in camp. Don't go near the minefield again."

"Okay, Top."

That wasn't the last time I got chewed out for doing what I thought was the right thing. I supposed that Top was right. Shit, he had survived two tours and was still alive to dress me down.

I didn't give much thought to the presentation ceremony that afternoon, but I did put that Buddha amulet around my neck and the prayer cloth in my left breast pocket. I'm not superstitious, but I thought it would help me bond with our mercenaries. I had no inkling that those icons might save my life.

Bunard

It was April 11, 1968, and I'd been in country for five months. The Mike Force had been summoned to A-Camp Bunard in the northwest corner of our Tactical Zone about 20 klicks from the Cambodian border, located adjacent to a road that was used by the North Vietnamese as a resupply route. Charlie was harassing the camp with mortar, rocket, and sniper fire. We choppered in two companies of our strikers and six Americans. Captain Rico Perez was with us, an operations officer from B-36, and close friend of Lauder, who was on R&R at the time. I had never been on an operation with Perez before, and didn't know what to expect. By rank he was the ad hoc commanding officer.

I had assumed that all Special Forces officers were seasoned warriors, but I had the sense that none of my other teammates were comfortable with Perez. The intelligence briefing suggested enemy elements were in the area. The plan was for us to run a search-and-destroy mission on the east side of the road, opposite the camp. Bunard would field two companies of Vietnamese CIDG, and would track our movements along the camp side of the road. Stevens was our company's CO and I was XO. Perez was along for the ride.

The terrain was hilly and the jungle thick with vegetation. Stands of bamboo made it difficult to gain ground. Visibility was poor. We hiked out about two klicks from camp before we crossed the road. Continuing about half a klick, we lined up our companies in two columns about 50 meters apart and proceeded to track the road as it headed toward Cambodia. We wanted to cover about five klicks per day, and figured we'd be in the jungle for about a week.

After stopping for a chow break at about 1300 hours, we got under way only to make contact with an estimated company-size NVA element. I was near the front of the column with Perez. Stevens was in the other column and radioed me to close ranks with him.

The AK-47 fire was heating up as we closed in on the enemy. We hit the deck as the bullets were slamming into trees and vegetation all around us. Typical of our operations, we would drop and reconnoiter the situation to determine our tactical approach on the enemy's position. We then would radio the camp to alert our artillery. Rather than dropping to the jungle floor, Perez bolted in the direction of the shooting, like he was on a mission! Assuming he knew what he was doing, I got up on my hands and knees to follow him, and there was an immediate burst of live-fire coming from close in.

Perez screamed, "MEDIC, MEDIC. I'M HIT."

Simultaneously, I felt a punch in my chest and a burning sensation, like someone had touched me with a hot poker. I didn't give it any thought and ran one more step, but tripped on tree roots and landed face first on the jungle floor. The chaos of the firefight made focusing difficult, and I had to keep my head down or else get it blown off.

"MEDIC! MEDIC! MEDIC!"

I remember swearing at Perez under my breath: shut the fuck up. You'll get us both killed, but he continued screaming. My chest burned. I did a push-up in the vegetation, high enough to see a hole in my fatigue shirt, but I didn't think much of it. I thought it might have been a fragment off a tree, or a branch that had been shattered by machine gun fire. But I was in pain and had to make sure that whatever it was hadn't broken skin. I unbuttoned the shirt and there was a hole about the size of a fountain pen barrel in my chest, blood bubbling with every one of my breaths.

Fuck. I've been hit, but by what? I was dumbfounded. I knew what an AK-47 bullet could do. I knew it had to be an AK; it was the NVA's standard issue weapon. It wasn't one of ours. I looked again at my wound. The bullet had entered my chest about two inches from the center of my sternum, over my heart. Jesus Christ! But I'm still alive! If that had been an AK fired at point-blank range, I'd be on the fucking ground with a hole the size of a baseball in my back, bleeding out. But I wasn't. All I could think was that the bullet had ricocheted off a tree, or maybe it went through Perez first.

I had a sucking chest wound and I was bleeding internally. I cursed at Perez under my breath. Fucking asshole. Why did I follow him? Yelling and screaming for his life, he didn't even know my name. What kind of Special Forces soldier was he? A pussy, a wannabe, an officer desk jockey out in the field to qualify for a Combat Infantryman Badge or grandstand for a medal. I wanted him to die so the firing would stop. Die, you fucker. I'm not coming after you.

"What the fuck's going on, Pete?" yelled Stevens over the radio.

"Perez is hit. I was behind him before he bolted. He just took off ahead of me."

"Why the fuck did he run up there?"

"I have no idea," I gasped.

"MEDIC! MEDIC! I'M HIT! MEDIC! MEDIC!" Perez's bloodcurdling screams echoed through the jungle.

The AK-47s responded.

Stevens yelled: "McShane, go up and get him."

I thought about it for a split second. I knew I needed to go up and tend to Perez, but I didn't want to, that fucker.

"I'm hit, too."

I tried to put a compress on over the hole in my chest before my lung collapsed, but the bandage wouldn't stay put. I tossed it aside.

"Stevens, I'll grab Asi and he can help me tend to Perez."

By now, Stevens had made it over to my column and was behind me. The Cambodes lay down a field of fire so Asi and I could low crawl up far enough to get to Perez. Adrenaline coursed through my body as we crawled along the jungle floor. My chest ached, and I had trouble breathing. Moving my left arm caused shooting pain through my chest. The air around us vibrated with the chatter of rifle fire. The chaos of the firefight swallowed us up. We crawled about 10 feet to where Perez lay motionless, lying with his face plugged into the jungle floor, body twisted over jungle roots. The NVA relentlessly pounded us, making it difficult to gain ground. Now that I could see him, I yelled to Stevens to call in an artillery strike and in a matter of two minutes the ground ahead of us quaked with 105s from Bunard. The explosions flooded the area with the acrid smell of cordite, burning my nostrils and throat, making it more difficult to draw a breath. Smoke swallowed the battlefield. I was terrified, yet the incoming rounds gave me a sense of relief knowing that they would take out some of the NVA, who at this point were on top of us. After 10 artillery rounds, the relentless pounding of the AKs trailed off but didn't stop. I could still hear pops all over the landscape.

I could feel blood gurgling in my chest. Breathing was excruciatingly painful, every breath like a dagger plunged to the hilt. My left lung collapsed as blood filled my chest cavity. My pulse was weak and breathing shallow: I was going into shock. I couldn't lie down, or I'd choke on my own blood. I asked Asi to start an IV on me.

Perez had taken two rounds in the gut and one in the elbow; his arm dangled. Over the course of the next 30 minutes, Asi and I treated him and 15 of our Cambodes, while the firing continued.

Stevens called for a medevac chopper and in a matter of 20 minutes the strikers set up a perimeter and had a 30-meter circle cut in the bamboo suitable for a makeshift LZ.

In the lull of the moment, waiting for the skinship, I kept an eye on Perez, who was unconscious. I didn't know whether he'd make it. In the fog of battle, I never considered that I would die, never allowed myself to think about it, although, I knew that I had limited time to get to the MASH. I sat on the ground with my back against a tree and reality set in. The bullet must have grazed my heart, missing the folded Buddhist prayer cloth in my pocket. I remembered what Noh the elder had said, that it would keep me safe. Stevens looked at the hole in my chest.

"McShane, you are one lucky son of a bitch."

"I would have been luckier had Perez not been on this mission."

"Yeah, and I was just getting to like you!"

The medevac chopper couldn't land because the enemy was active and shooting. Instead, hovering overhead, they dropped McGuire rigs. As we lifted off the ground, I thought that they'd haul us into the chopper, but the winch malfunctioned. We dangled 60 feet below the chopper as it gained altitude, fresh targets for the enemy in the carnival of violence below. As I looked down at the jungle canopy, swinging at the end of the nylon strap, I saw muzzle flashes coming from the direction of the enemy's position. They were aimed at Perez and me. I had visions of AK rounds pounding my flesh, little volcanoes erupting with blood and sinew and bone, returning my essence to the earth below. The blades of the chopper seemed to move in slow motion. I looked over at Perez, unconscious, his body spinning at the end of his strap as if some unseen hand had set him in motion. The chopper was now out of range; my mind raced as I held my arms out like wings. I remembered the exhilaration of my first parachute jump and thought about how wonderful it would feel to fly effortlessly through the air. I was tethered at the end of some child's kite string, my body fluttering in the wind, my spirit soaring. I could see the horizon in panoramic view, the beauty of the lush green countryside, the edge of the azure sky where it settled on the horizon a million miles away. Livestock grazed below and farmers went about their business tending to their fields, oblivious to my aerial performance.

Somehow we cleared the battlefield without being hit. The trip to the MASH hospital in Bien Hoa took about 20 minutes. Perez and I were now inside the chopper. He was on a stretcher, and I was sitting up. The chopper medic tried to persuade me to lie down on a stretcher, but I could feel the pressure of my own blood, taste it, and felt like I'd drown if I did. When we landed at the MASH, I staggered off the chopper carrying my IV bottle, the chopper medic holding me up under my right arm. Aides ran up to meet us with a wheelchair and I collapsed into it.

The triage nurse immediately rolled me over to the OR prep room, where there were a dozen gurneys with guys like me, some groaning, others unconscious. It was a sea of bloody, twisted bodies. Fluorescent bulbs hanging from the ceiling flickered with the drone of the huge generator outside the makeshift array of temporary buildings and tents that was the MASH. The nurse told me I had to lie down, and I tried to explain why I couldn't. She gave me a shot of Demerol in my IV to ease the pain and with several orderlies, helped me onto a gurney, removing my bloody shirt before I lay down. They cut the rest of my tiger stripes off with scissors, but I held onto my Mike Force scarf with a death grip.

"Relax, soldier, your scarf is safe. We'll put it with your personal effects."

The ceiling began to move and the whole scene blurred as the pain medication took hold. I thought about my teammates in that firefight and wondered how Perez was doing. I thought about my mother and father, our Sunday dinners and trips to grandma's and wondered whether I would ever see them again. I remember being lifted onto the operating table and being prepped for surgery. The surgeon looked at the hole in my chest, and then rolled me over to see if there was an exit wound.

"You're one lucky guy, soldier. That bullet missed your heart by a few millimeters. We're going to open up your chest cavity, fix what's broken and remove that bullet."

Just then, the anesthesiologist pumped a syringe of sodium pentothal into my IV and I blacked out.

I WOKE UP THE NEXT DAY in a hospital bed, dazed and in pain. There was a vacuum tube coming out of my chest between two ribs to keep my lung from collapsing. Drainage from my lungs came out the tube and collected in a glass jar on the floor beside my bed. The surgeons couldn't reach the bullet from the incision in the front of my chest. Three days later, I underwent a second surgery on my backside to remove the bullet and finish repairing the damage done to my lungs.

When I was well enough to travel, they medevaced me to Camp Zama, Japan, for further treatment and observation. The doctor came in one morning and removed the dressings to take a look. After asking me how I felt, he told me that my wounds were serious enough to send me back to the States to convalesce. He studied my record.

"Special Forces—McShane, I suppose you want to go back to your Team?"

Does he think I'm well enough to go back to my team? Why would he ask me if he knew I wasn't? I had been worried about this since my mind had cleared of the painkillers. I felt a tremendous sense of responsibility to not turn my back on my teammates, but I wondered how many more times I could cheat the gods before I lost. The medics before me weren't so lucky. I thought about how close that bullet had come to my heart and wondered whether God had sent me a message. Running around the jungle with that ragtag bunch of strikers was a surefire way to get killed. Stevens is right: I'm a lucky son of a bitch.

"No, not especially. I've had enough."

"Okay, soldier. We'll get the paperwork together and cut your orders. You'll be transferred to the military hospital nearest your home."

Two weeks after getting wounded, I was an inpatient at St. Albans Naval Hospital in Queens, New York. I spent the next five months convalescing.

St. Albans

By the time I arrived at St. Albans Naval Hospital, my sutures had been removed, but 18 inches of scars were stiff and raw, chest muscles sore, and my damaged lung scarred. Taking a breath felt like inhaling against a bear hug. Rehab consisted of stretching the chest musculature and doing upper body exercises with dumbbells, followed by deep breathing with a nebulizer. A week after arriving, the docs thought I was making good progress and issued me a 30-day leave, with instructions to continue my rehab routine. I could have gone anywhere, but I owed my parents a visit. My buddy Tuna came down in his '65 Corvette to pick me up. I felt oddly uncomfortable with him. I'd known him for six years, considered him my best friend, but riding in that car, I realized we had a lot less in common than I thought. He did most of the talking on the ride home; it was like I had never left—the same old shit about his pain-in-the-ass brother, asshole boss, and the search for a piece of ass. I zoned out, top down in the Vette, mid-May weather, trees and flowers in bloom, a welcome relief from the intrusive memories of

Vietnam. I felt like a selfish coward for having turned my back on my teammates. I had questions about my performance, whether I had done a good job. The only good thing about that leave was the little royal blue '65 Austin-Healy Sprite I bought. It gave me a lift, a diversion just when I needed one most. I drove it back to Albans and played with it all summer.

The thought must have been that I would relax and recuperate faster at home. The only rehab was going out to the bars every night. Drinking helped to dull feelings of guilt and inadequacy, but they came back with a vengeance in the morning, along with crushing headaches. My parents treaded lightly. I was distracted, disconnected from their daily lives, a son who wasn't home at home. I didn't know what to say, and they didn't know what to ask. There was no certainty in my life. I had no idea how long I'd be at Albans, nothing to look forward to except perhaps the end of my enlistment the following March. I was living in the here and now, as in Vietnam, but no one was trying to do me in, except perhaps me.

Back at the hospital, between rehab appointments, I had a four-hour afternoon shift as a hall guard in the hospital lobby. I stood near a pillar in my war suit, beret, and airborne jump boots, presumably to prevent commotions and otherwise act as a deterrent to any would-be crank looking for trouble. I didn't have a weapon, and can't remember whether they gave me a nightstick, but I had no idea what I would have done in the event of trouble. It was demeaning. I was the anomalous "Fighting Soldier from the Sky", on display in a naval hospital. Oh look, it's a Green Beret. Why is he here? I was one of only a few Army patients in a hospital ward full of Jarheads.

Marines are a different breed. There were seriously wounded among them: multiple amputation and disfiguring scars; crutches, canes, and wheelchairs everywhere. They were a determined bunch that thrived on one another's company. Proud and loud, it was nothing but bravado and ball busting on anyone who wasn't a Marine. I dished it right back and we became buddies in no time. There was a group of us who went out drinking most evenings trying to find our civilian lives, but all we talked about was military shit, like how bad C-rats were, asshole officers, and shitty field conditions, all things we had in common. Many of these guys were at Khe Sanh, a veritable three-month-long hell with incessant poundings from NVA artillery, rockets, mortars, and rifle fire. There was an SF camp there and I found out later that several of my medic classmates served there, saving Marine lives.

Some of the guys had serious anger management issues. Add lots of alcohol, and you had the makings of a volatile evening. We'd no sooner file into a bar down the street from the hospital than one of our guys would pick a fight with a townie. I was the mediator most nights, being the elder statesman at 24. Most of the Marines were barely out of their teens.

Over the summer, I brought some of the guys up to my family's summer cottage on Sandy Pond, off Lake Ontario, about 50 miles north of Syracuse. We'd hit all the summer gin mills and stay drunk all weekend, frolic in the warm freshwater surf, and sunbathe on the sandy beaches.

Before the summer was over, the docs said that my lung was as good as it was going to get. The scar tissue was permanent and my lung capacity diminished as a result. They gave me the option of going back to active duty, or taking a medical discharge. With under seven months left on my enlistment, Vietnam was out because there wasn't enough time for a full tour. A medical discharge sounded attractive, but I was told it would take at least six months to process, maybe eight. The prospect of spending those months at Albans was not appealing, nor was spending a day more in the service than I had to. If I couldn't go back to SF, I'd go the medical discharge route.

I met with an army liaison officer and talked to him about my options. A few days later he told me I could transfer to the 10th Special Forces Group at Fort Devens, Massachusetts. It was about an hour's drive from Boston, and 300 miles from Syracuse. Within a week, I was on my way to Fort Devens.

10th Special Forces Group

Jo and I met in Fall 1968 while I was stationed at Fort Devens, my last duty station. I'll never forget that night at The Mohawk, a club outside Fitchburg. It had a dance floor the size of a basketball court inside a converted warehouse, and on weekend evenings during the school year was packed with college women. A DJ played all the contemporary music, from the Beatles to Neil Diamond. I was there on a Friday evening with Fenster and Gildy, a couple of buddies from Devens, standing against the wall near the women's restroom. Jo was coming off the dance floor with another girl. Man, was she stacked, and beautiful to boot. A brunette, about five-seven, she wore a mini-skirt and cashmere sweater. As the two of them walked by us, I extended my foot and she tripped. Running to her side, I grabbed her by the shoulders and helped her to her feet.

"I'm sorry. It's really crowded in here. I apologize. Are you okay?" I said.

It took her a few seconds to regain her composure.

"A, yeah … I'm okay. Wow, that was close. I could have taken a header."

"Thankfully you're not hurt."

A few seconds passed while we looked at one another.

"My name's Pete," I said, and extended my hand.

She smiled, her cool blue eyes bright and inviting.

"I'm Jo, and this is Maureen." Her friend looked a bit perplexed.

Maureen was pretty, with dark curly hair and a fair complexion. She definitely was not the leader in this twosome. Jo had bearing, confidence. Maureen took her cues from her. I liked that.

Losing You played in the background.

"My pleasure. Hey, the least I can do is buy you ladies a drink."

She smiled and glanced at Maureen.

"Sure. Scotch on the rocks for both of us."

I caught the attention of a waiter.

"Garçon! A tray of scotch on the rocks, s'il vous plaît."

They laughed.

By the time the girls came back from the restroom, the drinks had been delivered.

I passed the tray to Jo and Maureen, then my buddies.

"A toast: to two beautiful women in a clutch of thorns."

We all had a good laugh. Fenster began talking with Maureen.

Jo took another sip of her drink.

Kentucky Woman boomed from the opposite end of the dancehall.

"So, do you go to school?" she asked.

I thought for a minute, not sure how to answer.

"Yes. A … R … M … Y."

Fenster almost choked on his drink before Jo got it. Then she laughed hysterically.

"Well, I can't top that," she said. "I'm just a nursing student. I graduate next June."

We carried on with small talk, but the music was speaking to me. I wanted to dance with this woman. The DJ put *Hey Jude* on the turntable. I grabbed Jo's hand.

"May I have this dance?"

She nodded and smiled. We danced that dance, and a half dozen more without saying a word. There was chemistry—it was visceral. Jo was provocative. Her energy pulsed through my body. At the end of the evening, we rushed outside to the parking lot and over to her VW Bug. We kissed and groped each other and gave in to our passion, rocking that car from side to side. For weeks, it continued in her VW or my Sprite, one of the smallest cars on the planet. Another time on a date, I drove her home after an evening of dancing, and we did it on the living room floor at the foot of the stairs to her parents' bedroom. She took risks like I did. Exhausted after lovemaking, we'd laugh like kids. She was the best thing about my last few months in the service.

Fort Devens, home to the 10th Special Forces Group, was a remnant of the First World War, with wooden barracks, tree-lined streets, and stately homes surrounding a grassy parade field. It had the classic feel of a New England town, understated, well-worn and comforting. I ran the Post Dispensary for the six months left of my enlistment. Devens felt safe, a welcome change from Nam, but it was total and complete boredom. I was anxious and depressed, guilt-ridden for having abandoned my Team, thinking that I hadn't done enough for our Cambodes, and the villagers near our camp. But how could I? I couldn't possibly handle all that by myself. There weren't any other medics to share the burden. I partied every night and most mornings struggled to open the dispensary at 0700. After morning sick call, I would catch a few winks on one of the hospital beds in the ward.

By November, I had already received my Purple Heart, and the Combat Infantryman Badge, instead of the traditional Combat Medics Badge. While I should have been flattered that my teammates thought enough of me to acknowledge my role as a tactical leader, I felt cheated. I hadn't received any information about the Silver Star Award I was told Lauder had recommended, so I sent a letter to the Awards Officer at the 5th Special Forces Group in Vietnam. Three weeks later, a reply stated that there was no record of the award. I was pissed. How could this be? Our Company Executive Officer, Rich Rees, told me personally that he and Lauder had each submitted me for the award. I wondered if some desk jockey had lost the recommendation, or rejected it because I hadn't done a good enough job.

Thinking about the army made me angry; I railed against the arcane military caste system and bullshit routines, the ineptitude of some officers and NCOs who lost records, delayed promotions, and took advantage of lower ranking enlisted personnel. Added to the list was the government and our gutless politicians, few of whom had ever been in the military or experienced firsthand the devastation of war. I thought about Perez and the firefight and couldn't believe I had survived. I thought I had fucked up, that I was to blame for getting myself shot. I should have known better. I would never have considered that a Special Forces officer could be inept. If he was, what would that have said about me? I took the blame.

Short-timers count the days and hours before separation. My last day in the service was March 10, 1969. The plan was to drive by the commanding general's office and present him with my final salute—a double flip of the bird. When the day finally came, I drove straight off post as fast as I could and onto the highway home, a civilian at last. But I didn't feel emancipated. There was an emptiness, as if I had left the better part of myself back in the army still connected to my team.

In May, two months after leaving the service, a manila envelope arrived at my home from Military Headquarters, 5th Special Forces, Republic of Vietnam. It had been a year and a month since Bunard, and I thought that maybe it was news of my Silver Star. I anxiously opened the envelope and pulled out the orders only to find that the award had been downgraded to a Bronze Star with "V" Device for Valor. This was confirmation that I had fucked up on that operation, that I shouldn't have hesitated when Perez screamed for help, that I should have known better than to follow him, even though he was a captain, an officer, and acting company commander. I shouldn't have assumed that he knew what he was doing. I was devastated. Now I had all the proof I needed—I was a failure.

I spent the summer partying, trying to forget. When I was drunk, I felt like I had no limitations, but the hangovers brought me back to reality in a hurry. I'd joke with my friends about the scars on my body, how close I had come to getting greased, as if it was no big deal. Those scars were my badge of courage. I found myself searching for excitement, for thrills, taking risks that perhaps might duplicate the exhilaration of a firefight. I'd pass on the double yellow line, race speedboats and fast cars, but never come close to the risks I took in war. When Charlie took a shot at me there was a risk of dying, and I had no control over it. When I'd drive fast, or take risks passing with oncoming traffic, I had total control over the event, and at the precise moment when the threat of dying was imminent, I'd back off. There is no backing off in war. Yes, I missed the adrenalin rush but I had no interest in going back to Vietnam.

I saw a lot of Jo over that summer. When I was with her, I felt like I had a purpose, a reason to push forward, to take my mind off the past. We talked about the future, our dreams and aspirations. I loved her. I remember giving her an engagement ring as she bent over to pick up potatoes out of a bin in her parents' root cellar one Saturday afternoon in July. I held the ring in front of her eyes as she was picking the potatoes out of a bushel basket. She screamed and the potatoes went flying, then she turned and hugged me as hard as she could, saying yes … yes … yes.

Part II

THE WAR ZONE AT HOME

Back on Campus

There was never a question what I would do for a living after leaving the service. I was obsessed with becoming a doctor—a healer, a saver of lives. My dream was to become a GP and work with underserved people. I knew I wouldn't make a lot of money, but that wasn't important to me. As Jo and I planned for our life together in the summer of 1969, we decided to live in Syracuse, and I would take an evening course that fall at the university to get my mind back into the swing of collegiate academics. I had been accepted at Syracuse University as a second-semester sophomore beginning in the spring of 1970. My war wounds had earned me a 40 percent disability rating from the Veterans Administration, and that qualified me for the Vocational Rehabilitation Program, a full ride right through medical school, my tuition and books paid for by the government. I would receive a monthly subsistence payment to cover food, clothing, and other necessities. It was only around two hundred dollars. Jo would have to work. She had graduated from nursing school, and we didn't think she'd have any trouble finding work in Syracuse. Jo and I married in November.

I had tried to get a job at Eastern Ambulance Service as an attendant, what is now referred to as an EMT. I made an appointment with the owner of the company, a Mr. Jordan. His office was in an industrial building where his ambulances were serviced and stored. I walked in through a huge garage door off the street. The coaches were parked diagonally against the two long walls of the building, and there was one idling in the doorway, the driver and attendant preparing to rush out on a call. Mr. Jordan's office was inside the door to the left, and as I entered, a siren went off as the ambulance came to life and rushed out onto the street. Two desks and several file cabinets were crammed into an office the size of a small bedroom. There was clutter everywhere: on the desktops, on top of the file cabinets and a windowsill looking out over a sidewalk. It didn't look like the office of a company president.

"Come in, come in. You must be Mr. McShane."

"Yes, sir, Mr. Jordan."

I had called him earlier in the week to ask about the possibility of employment.

"Please sit," as he got up and pulled an old wooden chair from the back corner of the room and placed it next to his desk. It was the only chair that wasn't covered in paperwork.

"So, you're interested in a job as an attendant?"

"Yes, sir."

"Okay. Do you have experience?"

I handed him my resume. The only work experience was summer jobs at the steel mill, and my military experience as a Special Forces Medic. The expression on Jordan's face changed as he spent a few seconds reviewing it. He took the cigar out of his mouth and looked up at me.

"You don't have experience as an attendant?"

"Mr. Jordan, I was a combat medic, trained in trauma medicine."

Now he looked confused.

"I don't get the connection. This isn't a war zone, Peter. Our job is pretty simple. We bring people to the hospital. Some of them may be accident victims, but we don't render treatment."

"Mr. Jordan, the connection is that I know how to keep people alive. I went through almost a year of training to learn how to do that, and I have practical field experience."

He tapped his cigar on an ashtray that looked like a tire off a lawnmower and stuck it back between his lips.

"Look, son, I can appreciate your position. In order for me to hire you, I need to make sure that you can do the job. You would need to get New York State certified as an attendant, and that could take up to a year. I could cover the cost of the training and give you a job as a driver in the meantime, if you would be interested."

My heart skipped a beat as his words worked their way around the cigar. I thought this would be a sure thing. I could feel my face get hot, but I wasn't in the mood to argue with him. I knew I could do the job.

"Thanks, Mr. Jordan, but I'm going back to college in the spring, and I wouldn't be able to work full-time, anyway."

He almost looked relieved.

"I appreciate your honesty," and he stood to shake my hand. As I walked out of his office, I felt like slamming his door, and remembered what they told us in the army exit interview—your skills are transferable. There was no comparable civilian occupation back in 1969 for me to pursue. I had heard something about a Physician Assistant program at Duke University, but there was no program offered anywhere in New York State. Besides, I wanted to become a medical doctor, nothing less.

While I was in the Army, my mother used to send me the St. John Fisher College newsletter to keep up with the lives of my former classmates. Frankly, it pissed me off, but maybe that's why she did it. If I had stayed in school and not enlisted, it might have been a story about me getting into medical school. Instead, it depressed me. I wanted to send all of my former classmates' pictures of the wounded guys at St. Albans, the ones with no legs, no arms, and no future and tell them that if it wasn't for us, they might not have been able to finish college.

I didn't realize how good I had it at John Fisher until I got to Syracuse University.

Signing up for classes at Fisher was easy; my class advisor took care of it. Professors knew each student by name, and they were accessible. Classes were small, and if you needed help, it was there. Another relationship that I never took seriously and squandered was that the Dean of Students, Father Joe Dorsey, had been my father's roommate at St. Michael's College in Toronto.

Signing up for classes at SU was the first sign that things would be different. In the College of Liberal Arts, you went to the women's gym, where an endless row of tables stretched wall to wall with the courses available for the semester. Students ran from line to line trying to get into the courses they wanted. The lines were long, and if you didn't play the game, you'd get shut out of the best courses, simple as that. If you were sick that day, too bad.

Many undergraduate level courses were held in auditoriums holding 300 students. Some classes were taught by Teaching Assistants, and you were lucky if you ever saw the professor, much less met him. Upper class courses were generally smaller, and TAs filled in if the professor was ill or away at a conference. It was a wholly impersonal experience, unless you were adept at manipulation, and willing to actively promote yourself with your professors.

The growing unrest over our presence in Vietnam was evident on the SU campus that spring, anger no doubt fueled by the disgrace of the My Lai massacre and the Kent State killings. The news media kept the spectacle of an unpopular war alive with graphic reports from the war zone. Students protested the war, held sit-ins and otherwise had little tolerance for any opposing viewpoint.

They desecrated the flag and carried effigies of soldiers, vilifying us as baby killers and warmongers. I wasn't spat upon or dissed, because I looked and dressed like a student. I grew my hair long and moved around campus incognito. But I felt like an amputee, cut adrift from the student body. No one knew I had been a soldier. As if I had a choice—run to Canada or get drafted. It would have taken more courage to run.

I'm sure there were other vets on campus but they were probably hiding, too. The protesters' arguments were logical and made me question our mission in Vietnam. Our government propped up a corrupt regime in South Vietnam under the guise of preventing the spread of communism. The US violated the Geneva Accords of 1954, which called for the unification of North and South. Elections never took place. I took a bullet for that. Confused and shaken, I wanted desperately to believe that my presence in Vietnam helped people, that I did some good. But embracing the protesters would have rendered my sacrifice, and those I had served with who died, meaningless.

I wanted them to know that I risked my life to rescue a child in a minefield, that I had doctored hundreds of local villagers who had never in their lives had professional medical care, that I never knowingly took another person's life in a firefight.

Protesters weren't in a conciliatory mood and didn't want to hear my stories. We were both angry: they needed someone to blame for the collateral damage, the senseless, wanton slaying of innocent people in two countries that wanted to unite, and I hated them for blaming me.

I remember an episode in February. Students were wrapped in American flags, and some were stomping them on the ground. A guy in a short haircut, a dead giveaway for a ROTC student, bent over to pick up one of the flags, and began arguing with a couple of students who were hassling him. I had already made peace with myself, having decided that I would ignore the protests, but when

I saw this guy, I decided to do something about it. I walked over to the GI and when he was about to throw a punch at one of his interrogators, I grabbed his arm and pulled him off balance toward me.

"Bro, let's get out of here. This is a no-win situation."

The guy looked at me like I was wacked.

"What the fuck are you doing, man? Those pussies deserve to be creamed."

"That's just what they want you to do, soldier. I'm saving you for another day. Pick your battles."

The GI looked disoriented, then came to his senses.

"Mind your own business," he said, yanked his arm out of my grip, and without a word went on his way.

Once Nixon authorized the Cambodian invasion on April 30th, college campuses exploded in violence. The Kent State killings by National Guard troops in early May precipitated student riots and picketing at colleges all around the country. A handful of radicals barricaded the SU campus and took over the administration building, holding the chancellor hostage and virtually shutting us down. The school closed early for the semester and there were no final exams. I was off to a bad start.

Big Decision

I settled into college life with determination, but it was a difficult transition for me, not just because of the antiwar sentiment on campus, which was palpable every day, but the impersonal nature of the educational experience. I was floating on a sea of hope, competing with thousands of other students, truly on my own. It was up to me to get the most out of my education.

I carried 17 credit hours that semester, a heavy load considering I had been away from college for five years. I declared Zoology as a major because it was a curriculum focused on the biological sciences, not one with concentrations in chemistry, which was SUs premed course. I remember having struggled with Chemistry at Fisher, and I would struggle with it at SU. It was an introductory-level course taught in an auditorium, a well-organized mill because it was required for all science curricula. The professor used an overhead projector and two huge chalkboards to make his points. It was easy to get distracted in such a large room, daydream about this or that, and you weren't missed if you didn't show up. Some of the premed students could be seen after class up at the front of the lecture hall kibitzing with the professor, asking for extra work, or otherwise making a nuisance of themselves. It used to turn my stomach watching them, but it paid off. Those students were the ones who got the As. I felt funny about begging for a grade. I wanted to work for it fair and square.

It took months to get into the academic groove. When I first enrolled at SU, I was able to transfer 40 credit hours from Fisher, most at a C-grade point, all I had to show for two years of effort. I was embarrassed. That first semester at SU was awkward. I was 25, married, the adult in a world of children. I was there to get a degree, period, not to protest, party, or skip class. It was business for me, something you did because you had to in order to get into the workforce.

I was driven, but it wasn't enough. I only pulled a C in Chemistry. I got a B in Embryology and an A in its lab, Bs in Economics and American History, and a C in American Literature, not a stellar GPA for someone interested in medical school.

Jo was working on the IV team at Crouse Hospital. We were on a waiting list for Married Student Housing, which offered subsidized rent for student couples. MSH was filled with couples like Jo and me, many with kids, so the sound of Hot Wheels careening down the sloping sidewalk outside our bedroom window at seven thirty Saturday morning after a night of drinking was a rude wakeup call. We made many friends there, all of us in the same boat, so to speak; future lawyers, accountants, district attorneys, professors, and deans of students. Our life there helped to balance my frustration competing with students younger than me, most coddled and privileged, whom I resented.

THE FALL SEMESTER OF 1970 started out like the spring semester had ended with student protests, but I simply ignored them. I was on a mission to get an education and get the hell on with my life. My junior year in 1970-71 was all science: organic chemistry, physiology, and genetics, each with labs, vertebrate morphology and evolution, and animal behavior. When I wasn't in class or lab, I studied constantly. A lighter load would have made more sense, but I wanted to finish my degree as soon as possible, and my grades suffered. I got Bs and Cs in my major, and struggled with organic chemistry, only pulling a C, a disappointment. As the year progressed, I became concerned whether medical school was a realistic goal. I wanted nothing more than to become a doctor, and thought that my practical experience as a combat medic, plus maturity would be worth something to an admissions committee.

It became apparent that in my haste to get through SU as quickly as possible, I had jinxed myself. My poor Fisher grades didn't transfer well, either. I was sick about it, resentful at having to compete for the precious few seats in medical school with younger students who had better academic records, angry with some of them who I thought didn't deserve the grades they had begged for.

One option I had considered was going to grad school for a master's in Microbiology in an effort to gain entrance to medical school. It would mean another two to three years of study. I was 26 at the end of my junior year, meaning that I'd be 29 or 30 before starting medical school. I was despondent. The thought of another seven or eight years of additional school with internship and residency was daunting, weighing heavily on my mind. I tried to see myself as a full-time student in my thirties and imagine what strain it would put on my relationship with Jo. And I was concerned that I might not be able to hack med school academics.

My Uncle Frank, a country doctor near Asheville, North Carolina, had offered to help me get into med school. He followed his father into his medical practice, but his passion was Duke basketball, golf, and flying. He'd fly his twin-engine Piper Aztec up to Syracuse during the summer and take us flying. He had a beautiful custom-built home on a wooded lot, a new Cadillac every two years, and seemed to have it all, but his life wasn't his own. Whenever we visited, he was always working. Back then, he did everything from treating sore throats to delivering babies, with house calls in between. He seemed happy, but I never asked him whether he ever regretted his decision to go into medicine. His escapes were his passions. I wondered whether I'd be happy practicing medicine.

But practicing medicine was my life's work. I knew I'd be good at it because I was good at it in Vietnam. It was the only part about my Vietnam experience that fulfilled me. I loved helping other people, but Jo didn't share my dream. Our limited income made it difficult to make ends meet. Without her support, I couldn't go to medical school.

Then the bombshell—Jo told me about how the interns and residents, even the married ones, used to solicit her and the other young nurses at the hospital. When we'd talk about med school, she'd cry uncontrollably.

"I don't want to lose you," she'd say.

She was convinced that I was going to dump her after she put me through med school. I spent months trying to calm her concerns, but I couldn't dissuade her. I had no intention of abandoning her, but there was nothing I could say to ameliorate her fear. I felt betrayed. She didn't trust me. A pall swept over our relationship, a creeping mistrust that threatened to devour our marriage. I was beside myself, torn between going for my dream, as I had in Special Forces, and embracing the love that had brought Jo and me together. She had grounded me at a time in my life when I was despondent and needed her love. I didn't want to lose that. I loved her and I could not, would not abandon her. I kept thinking about Uncle Frank and how it seemed that his hobbies were the only thing he really loved about his life. I tried to think about career options.

Vocational Rehab would pay for a master's degree, but in what? I was taking invertebrate zoology courses with a renowned Woods Hole researcher, W. D. Russell-Hunter, and I loved the courses. The thought of studying for a master's in this field appealed to me. I had done well in all my lab courses, but the thought of spending all my time in the lab as a researcher turned me off. I kept thinking about medicine and whether being a hospital administrator might be a reasonable compromise. There were schools around the country offering degrees focused on the discipline, master's in hospital administration, but not at SU. I decided that pursuing an MBA might open up possibilities for me in healthcare, even without an MHA. I was able to arrange internships with a local hospital as part of my MBA program. It focused on the operational and financial aspects of running a hospital: statistical analysis of patient admissions, collection of data, and generations of reports. It was tedious, mind-numbing work, and it had nothing to do with medicine.

I worked for two vice presidents during multiple internships; one was the operations manager and the other was the financial manager, and it gave me a firsthand look at politics in the business environment. Both men wanted to become the CEO, and tension was palpable.

During my final semester, I floated the idea of working for the hospital, but I had the sense that neither of them wanted me onboard. I think they were jealous because the president and chairman of the board liked me. It was clear that there would be no career for me in medicine.

My dream was dead.

I tried to focus on finishing my MBA degree as quickly as possible and getting into the workforce. I didn't know what I wanted to do, what career to pursue. I had never considered anything else. As the last semester wound down, I interviewed with a retail stock brokerage called duPont Glore Forgan & Co., recently purchased by H. Ross Perot. They invited me to Rochester for an interview with the branch manager.

I put on my polyester suit, patterned shirt, and zip-up boots, and walked into his office, a maze of glass cubicles in a huge building downtown. It was three o'clock in the afternoon, and other than a receptionist, there was no one else in the office. Stuart Wells, the branch manager, came to the door of his corner office and welcomed me. The office had a commanding view of the Rochester skyline. There was a leather couch, coffee table, modern office desk, matching credenza, leather desk chair, and three side chairs. The walnut paneling was rich looking, but there were no paintings or wall hangings of any sort. Several cardboard boxes sat on the floor and it looked like he had just moved in.

"Peter? I'm Stuart Wells. Welcome."

"Mr. Wells, my pleasure, sir."

The guy had a military haircut. I had grown mine long after leaving Fort Devens. A little research about DGF revealed that Perot had purchased the company after they were unable to meet a capital call by the SEC. Now he was changing the way they did business, running it like the military.

"So, McShane, you want to be a stockbroker?"

He caught me off guard. I wasn't sure I wanted to be a stockbroker.

"I'm interested in learning more about the job, Mr. Wells."

"Well, I can tell you, if you want to make a lot of money, this is the place. You can make a hundred grand a year in this business. In fact, if you were only making a hundred grand, I'd be upset with you. We expect a lot of our brokers."

I looked around at empty cubicles.

"How long have you had an office here, Mr. Wells?"

"We opened it three months ago. I'm up from Manhattan. I'm interviewing for brokers now. New recruits go to LA for a six-month training program to learn how Mr. Perot does things. He runs a tight ship."

"So, if I were to join the organization, I'd have to move to Rochester, right?"

"That's right."

"Do you pay moving expenses?"

"We do, but if you leave within two years, you promise to reimburse us a pro rata share of the expense; it's in the employment contract."

"I see."

"We work hard here. I'm here until seven or eight at night. Some nights I sleep on that couch," and he pointed to the leather couch I was sitting on.

"How many brokers work here?"

"We've got four in training and three here in this office; they're out on calls now that the market is closed."

"What's the next step?" I said.

"I'll send you an employment package with our benefits information, and an employment offer."

"Alright, I'll look forward to reviewing it."

"Are you looking at any other opportunities?"

"Yes, sir."

"Other brokerage companies?"

"No."

"Oh. Okay, I look forward to your reply. By the way, get rid of the polyester suit and the boots. We wear wool pinstripes and solids, and white button-down cotton shirts, starched. Get yourself a pair of wingtips, and we like our haircuts high and tight."

"Got it."

I walked out of his office rolling my eyes, thinking he's got to be kidding. Turned out that Perot was not successful in transforming the securities industry with Marine Corps sales training and management techniques. DGF went bust a year later in 1974.

My final interview was with First National City Bank, FNCB *a.k.a.* Citibank. I had not considered the banking business, because I thought of it as a retail business dealing with individuals, branch banks on every corner, and managers sitting in offices hidden behind potted ornamental trees and tellers' counters. FNCB was interviewing for commercial lending trainees to staff newly opened offices in upstate New York. I didn't know anything about making loans to businesses, but it sounded interesting.

The initial interview on campus lead to a day's worth of interviews with senior people in New York City at the bank's headquarters at 399 Park Avenue in midtown Manhattan. There were four of us from SU who were chosen for the second round of interviews, all but one were graduating MBAs. I was the only one who wasn't a finance or accounting major. In fact, I had had only one finance and one management accounting course; my major was operations management. They flew us down to New York together and we were met at the airport by a limousine and driven right to the front door of bank headquarters.

The building was impressive, overlooking the Park Avenue grass median and a short walk from Central Park. We were interviewed by each of the four regional presidents of the new upstate banks. I thought I did well with each of them, but I particularly liked the head guy in the Albany region, Bob Burns, a long-time employee. He was irreverent in a cocky sort of way, but very professional. He explained what we would be doing as lending officers, making loans to medium and large businesses, with sales up to $100 million. Companies larger than that would be referred to the corporate bankers in Manhattan.

After our individual interviews, we were addressed by the human resources manager who told us about the training program and what would be covered, and gave us some pointers as to appropriate dress, which included shined shoes and crisply starched shirts for the men. He followed by saying those who pass the interview phase would receive offer letters within a week.

I was excited as we boarded the limo for the trip to LaGuardia and the flight home. I told Jo about the trip and how exciting New York City was, even though we didn't spend any time outside of the bank that day. I told her that the training program was six months long, and at the end, we'd be assigned to one of the four regions:

Buffalo/Jamestown; Syracuse; Albany, and Mid-Hudson. We'd live in a subsidized apartment within walking distance of the bank. Jo had never been to the city, and we had our fingers crossed. The offer came the following week.

I had a good feeling that I was making the right decision about going into the banking business. I would be working for a first-class corporation and receive training in a profession that could open doors for me later on. And I thought that I'd be making money, a lot of money, which was what I wanted, fair recompense for giving up my dream. I accepted the FNCB offer and prepared to move to Manhattan in mid-June of 1973. I had completed the MBA course requirements in 12 months by taking day and evening courses and four courses in summer school.

The Banker

Jo was numb after almost four years supporting us. Our lives changed dramatically after we got married in November 1969. The adventurous, confident young woman became the breadwinner, and her self-confidence plummeted. We were strangers living in the same apartment. I learned that she had a short fuse and wasn't afraid to throw a dinner plate to make her point, but she never apologized, and we seldom reconciled after an argument—it was more like a truce. She was emotionally distant. When she said "I love you," it felt skin-deep. She wasn't a touchy-feely kind of person, and I am. Whether it was her work, my studying, leaving her family in Massachusetts, or lack of friends, she seemed more dependent on me, and I didn't have the time to spend with her. I studied constantly, obsessed with getting into med school, and then having to turn away from it. Things were changing. That spark that drew me to her was fading. I hoped that once I was finished with bank training and assigned to a permanent office, our relationship would improve.

I had hit it off with Bob Burns, the president from Albany, during the initial interview, and thought that he wanted me for his territory. I trailed two of his commercial loan officers in their daily duties during a trial week in Albany calling on customers, doing financial analysis and presenting credits to Burns or his vice president, Bob McCormick. I guess that Burns thought I was a good fit because at the conclusion of the course, I was assigned to the Albany office.

Jo and I were happy with the assignment. During OJT, the bank put us up at a local hotel and we had a chance to snoop around the area. Jo was especially happy because we would be halfway between the in-laws and the outlaws, hers in Chelmsford, Massachusetts, mine in Syracuse.

THE FIRST FEW MONTHS in Albany were a welcome relief—finished with school and training. It was so good to get out of the city, even though we had enjoyed it. Jo and I were small-town people, and being back in the country made us feel at home. When Jo got pregnant, I got to work getting the baby's room squared away with crib, dresser and changing table, playpen, and toys. It was the wife of one of my friends from the bank who threw a baby shower for her. Jo felt intimidated by some of the guys I worked with and their wives made her feel self-conscious. She had only graduated nursing school, wasn't a four-year college grad. She worked for a few months before the baby was born, but then retired. We felt strongly that she should stay at home with our children, at least until they were in school. She was a good mother, and I think this helped with her loneliness and long days. My days were filled with ramping up my new career.

Our first son, Keith, was born in September, 1974. I had great trepidation about being a father, didn't think I was ready, even at the age of 29. I kept thinking about my father and his "sink-or-swim" method of child rearing and was determined to participate in my son's life. We took Lamaze classes and I was present when Keith was born. It was an amazing experience for me, even though

I had participated in many births while serving in the military. It wasn't the same. This was my own flesh and blood—I was in love. I helped Jo bathe and clothe Keith, changed his messy diapers, fed him, and rocked him to sleep. It was magical watching him crawl, say "Da," and take his first steps. He was into everything and I couldn't get enough of him.

We lived in a townhouse in Voorheesville, a village southwest of Albany. This was the first time in our marriage where we could actually enjoy being a family. We didn't know anyone, and socialized only with some of the people I worked with at the bank. To say our home was spartan was an understatement. We had almost no furniture, and limited money to spend now that Jo wasn't working. We started going to auctions to buy furniture. We loved the look of period oak and walnut furniture and were lucky to find some nice pieces at reasonable prices. I took a night course at the local high school and learned how to cane chairs, so we got some great deals on antique chairs that needed help. I had always loved working with wood, so buying furniture that needed repair was a real money saver, and it fed my need to stay busy.

McCormick was a seasoned lending officer, having spent years in banking in and around the boroughs of New York. He was politically savvy and a first-class salesman. He and Burns taught me what it was like making loans to smaller businesses. They could read my detailed analyses and tell me what I had missed, what I had understated. It amazed me. Even though neither one of them were as well educated as I was, they had street smarts and ran circles around me when it came to sizing up a loan request. The sort of borrowers we found upstate were difficult to analyze with the stringent analytical procedures I had learned in training. The element that was missing was how to characterize the owner of a company and determine whether he was a man of his word. FNCB had no interest in making character loans, but this was the way the local banks had done business for a hundred years. If we were to compete with them, we would have to do the same. We were successful in booking new business, but it wasn't easy. The local banks were very competitive with loan pricing. They had flexibility where we didn't. We were often the high-priced guys. This forced us to look at deals that were sometimes hairy, borrowers who were being kicked out of the local bank, or who had reached the local bank's lending limit.

We had some wins and some losses. About a year later, the senior manager of the upstate expansion program was replaced by a guy from the National Banking Group named Rick Gilbert, a nervous guy with a speech impediment who was always "up". The guy worked from dawn to dusk, often slept in his office, and never came "down". He was on us constantly, and his man on the spot was a former classmate of mine from Fisher, a pudgy, arrogant jerk of a guy named Tim Coral. We used to make fun of him at college. He was a townie and when he visited us in the dorm, we'd bust his balls. He was the perfect complement to Gilbert, "Yes, Rick, no Rick," a follower with no backbone, and not an original thought in his head. He had an MBA from Notre Dame, and he thought very highly of himself, something he had learned rubbing shoulders with the prima donnas we had met in Manhattan during our training. We had some problem loans, and that's why Coral was sent up to replace Burns and McCormick, the "gun slingers".

We were told that we weren't selling the bank's philosophy properly, its strong suit—that Citibank was the "be all and end all of banking", so we all went back to school for a week to learn how to sell.

There were weekly reports to prepare for Coral, at which time he'd critique our performance. Of course, Coral was the expert when it came to making sales calls. He had all the answers, having been anointed by Gilbert, but when I brought him on joint calls, prospects were taken aback with his sanctimonious attitude. After all, we were in hayseed territory.

I was successful at bringing new business in the door, only to have it squashed, or priced so high that we'd lose the deal. Gilbert came up to the region regularly. On one trip, upset at our lack of progress, he dressed each one of us down.

"McShane, do you have a problem with Tim or me?"

I have a problem with both of you; you're company men.

"No, not especially."

"What do you mean?"

"Business in this market up here is different than down in the city. People don't respond to the marketing program. It's cold and impersonal."

"Oh, it is? What would you suggest?"

"I'd suggest that we take a page out of the local bank playbook and watch how they continue to hold on to their relationships despite our presence in the marketplace."

Gilbert's face turned red. He looked like he wanted to throttle me.

"McShane, I don't think you trust us. I don't think you trust me." He was indignant. "I'm going to test your trust from here on out. I want you to continue to follow our marketing plan, do you understand?"

"Yes, sir."

It was bullshit. I was the biggest producer in the office, but that lack of trust thing hit me between the eyes. Lack of trust? If anyone should have a lack of trust, it was me. I knew what I had to do, make a change, get away from this madness. The whole Citibank thing was anathema to me. They expected you to take on the persona of the bank, lose your identity as an individual. It was no better than a cult, and if you expected to advance in the ranks, you had better toe the line. Not me. I needed to formulate a plan to get out.

After that meeting, senior management changed again in New York, this time replacing the senior vice president with a marketing guy from Proctor and Gamble, the soap people. It was laughable. Before the changes took place, I attended a hospital administration conference at the Kutsher's, a conference center in the Catskills. Healthcare was a market segment in which we had expertise and an area of potential growth. I had a few too many Scotches that evening and was getting tired of Coral's incessant harping on the way that I conducted business.

"McShane, I think you need to change the way you do things. We're looking at too many companies who ultimately take our offers to their local bank to match."

"Tim, since you're the expert at sales in the office, why don't you tell me what I have to do to be more selective. Ask the prospect upfront if they're going to shop our deal?"

"Don't get snippy with me. I know what I'm talking about."

I looked at the pompous ass in front of me and wanted to pound him.

"When was the last time you brought a deal in, Tim?"

"That's enough, McShane. I think you've had too much to drink."

"Actually, Tim, I'm just getting warmed up."

His face flushed.

"If it wasn't for all the so-called dead beats I drag in the door, we wouldn't have any new business."

"I'm finished talking to you," he said. When he turned to walk away, I grabbed him by the sleeve of his coat and swung him around.

"I'm not finished talking with you. Who do you think you are? Can't you see what's going on out in the trenches? We're getting our asses kicked out there trying to do things the National Banking Group way. Don't you think it's time we talked about what we're doing wrong?"

"You can take it up with Gilbert on Monday. He'll have something to say about your behavior."

I lost it. I grabbed his shoulder and planted my right foot preparing to send a roundhouse fist to his face. Rick Samples, one of our other account officers, grabbed my arm before I could do any damage. Coral stood there, stunned.

"Let's you and me take a walk," said Samples as he led me down the corridor and into the barroom.

"Why the fuck did you stop me, Rick? I've wanted to do that ever since that asshole wannabe hung around my dorm at Fisher."

"Holy shit, man. You came close. No telling what he would have done had you hit him."

"I don't care. He's nothing but a fucking empty suit. They're all prima donnas smoking the Citibank dope."

I went to my room and slept it off. Next morning, I skipped all the meetings and went home early for the weekend. Monday came and went, and no one said a word about Thursday night.

FAMILY LIFE WAS THE ONLY respite I had. Keith turned two in September 1976, and he was more fun than I had ever imagined. We had a black Lab by then, and he would pull her jowls and laugh, while she'd shake her head in disgust. We'd play horsey and he'd beg for more. Jo was pregnant with our second son, Rich, who was due in January. We talked about what was going on at the bank, and she was supportive of moving, especially if it turned out to be Syracuse. Jo had made many friends while we were at SU. I would begin the job hunt after the baby was born. We decided to try the less-intrusive Leboyer birthing method, where, in a dimly lit room, the baby is delivered into a warm-water bath. Rich never cried as the doctor slipped him into the basin. I felt like crawling into the bath with him.

I sent letters of introduction to the three most prominent regional banks, including Lincoln First Bank in Rochester and Syracuse. I followed up with a phone call to speak to the President, Jim Balderston III, and he invited me to visit him at headquarters in Rochester. A week later, I had an offer to join the commercial lending department. I heard some years later that Gilbert had a heart attack and died face down at his desk early one Sunday morning, a loyal Citibank soldier. He was 46.

Trust

The interviews at Lincoln First Bank in March of 1977 went well. Balderston was a real gentleman, and his employees held him in high regard. A scholar-athlete and landed gentry, his family owned a significant interest in the bank, yet he didn't talk down to anyone. There were no outward signs of the snobbishness or trust issues I had experienced at Citibank. He gave me a choice of working in the corporate lending group in Rochester or Syracuse. After meeting both senior lending officers, it was a toss-up, but I opted for Syracuse. Jo and I were ecstatic. I got a $5,000 raise to $28,500, a title of Assistant Vice President, and they'd move us.

I started to commute from Albany in March. I only saw my family on weekends, and it was lonely. I missed them terribly. Jo had her hands full with a two-year-old and a newborn, but I had to work. The commuting would only last until we found a home in Syracuse.

I got a panic call at the office on a Monday in early April from Jo. She was sobbing. Rich had fallen from his changing table to the kitchen floor. She was on her way to the ER at St. Peter's Hospital in

Albany. I rushed to Albany immediately that morning. All I could think was that Rich was going to die, or have permanent brain damage. When I arrived at the hospital, he was in intensive care with a fractured skull. The neurologist said that there was mild swelling on the brain and that the next 48 hours were critical. Jo stayed at the hospital with Rich, while I went home to take care of Keith. By Saturday, the doctor said that Rich's swelling had gone down, and it would be okay to take him home on Sunday. With great trepidation, I went back to work the following Monday for the week, and Jo kept a close watch for any signs of trouble. We decided to house-hunt in earnest once Rich was stabilized in April, and found our dream home in one afternoon with the help of a realtor who was a friend and former neighbor of mine.

My boss was a recovering alcoholic named Bill Houck. Open and reflective about his drinking problem, he had worked for Chemical Bank in New York. He never intimated whether he had bailed from the bank or was fired, but after straightening himself out, he got a job as a CFO for a lumber mill in the Adirondacks. I don't remember how he wound up at Lincoln, but he was good at analyzing credits and good with the customers. At first I admired Bill, but there was something about him that bothered me.

When I first arrived at the bank, his boss, the senior lending officer, picked my brain about the systems and procedures at Citibank. He asked me to put together a weekly reporting procedure for every account officer as a way to track individual performance. There were other projects he gave me, including instituting a new business development program, but after a few months on the job, Bill began to badger me. He'd complain that I wasn't doing enough new business development myself, and that my write-ups were sloppy. At first, I took his comments seriously, but the annual review was a slap in the face. He told me I wasn't living up to my potential, that I needed to work harder. I began to think that Bill was jealous with all the attention the senior loan officer had showered on me. The smarmy son-of-a-bitch behaved like a typical dry drunk, irritable and demanding, behavior with which I was familiar because of my father's alcoholism. I'd fantasize about punishing Bill, arranging for him to break an arm or a few ribs accidentally tripping on a curb, or simply punching him in the face. I hated him. He didn't give a shit about me.

I had plenty to keep me distracted after hours. The house needed much updating: sanding floors, painting, and furniture restoration kept me sane during trying times. I never could relax, never wanted to relax. I guess you could say I was running, but I didn't know from what.

Jo and I connected with old friends and we were enjoying ourselves back in Syracuse, but the pall of my job weighed heavily on my mind. I wasn't happy. I hated politics, hated working for people who didn't have my best interest at heart, people I couldn't trust. My job put me in touch with scores of entrepreneurs. I felt the desire to be on my own in business, and I learned much from my customers. Rich was walking by then, and his older brother would play "Da" whenever I wasn't there. Rich didn't take well to his brother's "help". He was a single-minded child and preferred playing by himself. We'd spend weekends over the summer at my parents' cottage on Sandy Pond. I taught Keith how to fish, but it took him several years to hook his own worms. Both the boys were in water-baby classes at the YMCA, and they loved the beach in front of my parents' cottage.

It was about this time that I received a call from the regional vice president of Bankers Trust Company asking if I'd be interested in running the bank's region in Central New York, to take his place. I was flabbergasted. Was this too good to be true? Tom Clark had run the region for about five years, and had decided to leave banking for an opportunity to invest in a McDonald's franchise. We hit it off right away. I would have a $250,000 lending limit, the title of Regional Vice President, and a hefty raise, which brought my annual compensation to almost $40,000. I met the president of the bank and the credit department manager, Don Beard. He was a thin, pedantic little man with the nuanced voice of a radio announcer, modulated as if he were speaking to an audience. I think he liked to hear the sound of his own voice. I accepted the job, and Tom spent two weeks introducing me to all the commercial customers, then he was off to Hamburger University.

Right from the start, Beard was on my case. A micromanager, he didn't like my analysis, my credit write-ups, or the new customers I brought into the bank. In short, we didn't see eye to eye. Beard was the loan prevention department. He was a festering pustule on my back side. I despised him. It was a good thing that his office was in Utica. More than once, he pushed me to the brink with his idiosyncratic ranting about credit quality and attention to detail. And he'd say it in a measured monotone that I was a disappointment. If he wanted a fucking credit analyst, he should have hired one. I felt like putting my fist through his face.

Several months after I arrived, the bank president was hit by a cyclist while jogging near his Albany office, and died a day later. Once the dust settled, there was a complete reorganization of the bank and Beard was elevated to the role of senior lender. My new direct boss was a veteran lending officer and senior vice president named Al Higgins. It was then mid-1979. Al knew all about Beard and promised me that he wouldn't let him get in the way of me booking new business.

My long hours were affecting my relationship with Jo. I'd be out of the house at 5:45 a.m., off to the gym and wouldn't get home until 7:30 or 8:00 p.m., in time to tuck Keith and Rich into bed, and Jo would be frazzled. She was stretched to the breaking point, but so was I. The only emotional connection we had was our common love for our boys. There was no intimacy between us. I didn't know what to do about it except chug along and "provide" for my family.

The credit markets had tightened. Savings banks and S&Ls had gotten into the commercial lending market unprepared, and hundreds of millions in loans were defaulting. The prime rate had gone from 8 percent in January of 1978 to 15.25 percent by year-end 1979, peaking at 20 percent in April 1980. This put enormous pressure on businesses whose loans floated with the prime. Loan defaults surged. Al and I had an arrangement that I would bring in new business and he'd write up the deals. It worked for me, but Al was sloppy and his work was a reflection on me. This wasn't lost on Beard. Two of my customers had defaulted, one declaring bankruptcy. I could see one of them coming, but the bankruptcy was a surprise, and apparently, Al hadn't documented that deal, which I had booked in 1978, with his loan approval.

I was called on the carpet by the head of the commercial loan division, Jack Devan. Beard was not there, nor Higgins. Tom Boman, the bank attorney, was. I sat in front of Devan's desk. He had two files opened.

"I want to talk to you about Domtack, Inc. and Lomar. As you know, both of these loans are in default and Lomar has sought protection of the bankruptcy court."

He leafed through the pages, pausing a few times to look up at me.

"These are both weak credits, and there's no write-up on Lomar. Where is it? How could we have booked these transactions? These companies were in terrible shape!"

I couldn't understand why there was no documentation.

"I reviewed both of these deals with Al Higgins. They were both decent credits and he approved the loans. He told me he would do the Lomar write-up. That was our arrangement, so I could spend more time out on the street. I was buried in work. The borrowers are good people, and our prime was at 10 percent when we did those deals. No one knew that it would double within a year."

Devan looked drawn.

"These are shitty credits, and we're going to have to write them off. I blame you for this."

"With all due respect, Jack, it's not my fault that the prime went to 20 percent. This could have happened to any one of our customers."

"Why didn't you write up Lomar?"

"I told you. Al told me he'd take care of it. He had approved the loans. He told me he would do that write-up. Why didn't the credit department let me know that it was missing?"

"You're responsible for the credits in your region. I don't care what arrangement you had with Al."

"I'm sorry. I wasn't aware that Higgins never followed through."

"I'm sorry, too." He took a deep breath.

"We had high hopes for you. Unfortunately, you lack professionalism."

He had a determined look on his face as he took a breath.

"I'm going to give you two alternatives: either resign or I will fire you. The choice is yours."

I was still stumbling over the words lack professionalism when the words resign and fire hit me between the eyes. I didn't know what to say. It never occurred to me that I'd ever be fired. I thought I was doing a great job. Apparently, some people in the bank thought otherwise.

"What happened to my annual review? Al thought I was doing a great job."

"That doesn't change the decision."

"So I'm out?"

"Yes."

"When is this effective?"

"Immediately."

I had difficulty concentrating. I felt dizzy.

"What about a severance package?"

"If you resign, you'll get two months' pay and we'll carry your health insurance for four months."

He stood. The meeting was over.

"Think about it over the weekend and let Tom know your decision on Monday."

I walked out of the office oblivious to the surroundings, took the elevator to the exit for State Street, and walked out. I was numb, my feet on autopilot. I felt violated and self-conscious. The blur of people walking by me, the people next to me, they must know what just happened to me. Please explain it to me. Someone please tell me what just happened. I walked all the way up State to the Capitol building, about a quarter mile, turned and walked back down to where I had parked my car. I wonder if Higgins knows? That coward Beard. It's a good thing he wasn't in the meeting. I might have killed the fucker.

I stopped at the first rest area on the Thruway and called Jo on a pay phone.

"I was fucking fired today."

"Oh my God. What happened?"

"I got framed. That asshole Al Higgins never documented a deal last year and it went belly up. I think Don Beard finally got his wish. He's been gunning for me since the day I joined the bank."

"Just come home, honey, and please drive carefully."

The following Monday the bank attorney called and wanted to know what my decision was. I told him I thought that two months' severance was chintzy, and that I wanted four, with six months of health insurance. I could hear him huff on the other end. Later that day, he came back with three months' severance and six months health insurance.

"I'm going to prepare an agreement that I want you to sign."

"I'm not signing any agreement. You're going to have to take me at my word."

He was pissed, but he knew he could trust me. We had done a lot of business together in my time at the bank, and I thought we had a good relationship. Hell, I was the one who got him the position on our board of directors.

IT TOOK ME YEARS TO GET over the firing. It was deeply embarrassing, an affront to my self-image. I'd think about the problems I had at the other banks and how Don Beard just might have been right about me. I felt self-conscious whenever I saw a business associate or friend, anxious that they'd know what happened. My reaction to Beard and other bosses stirred up emotions that frightened me. The anger I felt was palpable, and it consumed me. I could have killed someone; I certainly knew how. I'd tell myself that there are assholes everywhere, that I wasn't the only one who had problems with superiors, but other people didn't cut and run. They put up with it for the sake of their families.

I began to think that I needed to get right with God. I hadn't gone to church since Army training, but I prayed constantly in Vietnam until I got wounded, then stopped. I didn't need to pray anymore. I had escaped death. I was invincible. No one could touch me. I was the master of my universe and didn't need God anymore. But with all that was happening in my life, the problems I had with trust, anger, and recurring feelings of guilt, I felt the need to let God back into my life. Memories of Vietnam made me think about the moral issues, what war does to innocent people, what we did to innocent people, and why I didn't do more to help those in need. I had tried to rationalize it, but couldn't.

Groveling for Cash

The first few months out on my own were scary, but liberating. I rented an office on the third floor of a charming, eighteenth-century stone building in Hanover Square in downtown Syracuse. The central business district in May of 1980 was in resurgence. Developers were taking advantage of public funding to restore historical buildings of significance. It was lonely, sitting at my desk in the back of the building next to a window overlooking the rear of another building, working on my only client's business, planning my marketing strategy, making calls to prospects. I made the rounds of all the accounting firms in town, offering to help clients who might be having trouble with their banks. The credit crisis fomented by the savings banks' burgeoning nonperforming loan portfolios had now spread to the commercial banks. While their loan portfolios were in much better shape, the bank regulators and auditors nonetheless scrutinized them. The banks dropped the hammer on troubled customers. They even kicked some out who were paying on time if the trends in their business were downward, or if they were in a troubled industry, like construction or restaurants. I made it a point to seek out these orphans and find specialized lenders who could meet their needs. I got to know asset-based lenders willing to take on more risk if they were able to collateralize a company's loans with buildings and equipment.

Our third son, Ben, was born in May just before I got fired. To add to the angst, the contractor who was remodeling our home went bankrupt and walked off the job. I spent the next two months finishing the work myself, installing a new built-in kitchen in the process. In December, Jo called me on my office phone, in distress.

"Ben just stopped breathing after his feeding. I thought he was napping. I shook him and yelled his name several times, and he finally gasped and took a breath."

She was hysterical.

"What if I had put him in his crib? Oh my God, he could have died."

"He didn't die, Jo. Get control of yourself. Call Pediatric Associates and get him in there immediately. I'll meet you there."

The pediatrician said that Ben had an episode of Sudden Infant Death Syndrome, and recommended we make an appointment to see an Upstate Medical University researcher who was an expert on SIDS. That evening, neither Jo nor I slept a wink, worrying that our Ben might die, but he slept quietly between us in bed. The next morning, we met with the doctor at Upstate and he confirmed our pediatrician's diagnosis. He suggested we enroll in a SIDS clinic at Strong Memorial Hospital in Rochester and have Ben's respiratory system evaluated. Within the week, the doctors there told us that the condition is typically caused by an immature respiratory system. Kids usually outgrow the condition by the time they're one year of age. The physical exam didn't uncover any irregularities or other conditions that might have caused Ben to stop breathing. They prescribed a halter monitor, a device with electrodes that could detect if Ben stopped breathing. He'd have to wear the device for at least six months; we did it for a year. Every day during naps and in the evening, we'd set up the machine, placing the electrodes on Ben's body, and we'd lie awake waiting for it to go off. And it did, frequently, but not because he stopped breathing. Rolling over from one side to the other would loosen an electrode, and the alarm would go off. It was nerve-wracking, especially for Jo. She was there on the front line during the day, while my head was buried in work.

On his first birthday, after a thorough examination at Strong, the doctors said that he was out of danger, and we were able to discontinue the monitor. But that didn't stop the worrying. It was always in the back of our minds.

My first year in business was a struggle. I hired a sales person who methodically canvassed the market for prospects, and hired my brother Matt, a Certified Public Accountant, to offer bookkeeping services. Cash flow was tight. Some weeks, there wasn't enough money to take a paycheck for myself, so I'd have to wait. I used my credit cards to cover groceries and auto loans. Before long, I was tapped out, and juggling bills by playing the float—paying bills with worthless checks in hopes that I could cover them before the checks cleared.

My relationship with Jo by now was platonic. She was not an intimate person, and the only time we seemed to make love was when she'd had a few drinks. Now, after my three aborted jobs in the banking business, she was concerned about our financial well-being. "At least with the banks, we had a steady paycheck," she'd say. She was raised in a conservative New England household where there were no credit cards or checking accounts—they paid cash for everything. When she found out that I was using credit cards to live on, she went berserk.

"What's wrong with you?" she shouted. "Why can't you just get a job like everyone else?" She stood in front of me with that determined look she'd get when she felt confident about her reasoning. Jo had a lot of common sense.

"Look. We've had this discussion before." She didn't understand risk-taking—the entrepreneur's mantra. A good business plan is essential, and I thought I had one.

"Yeah, the old 'I won't work for someone I can't trust'. Don't you care about our family? Don't you care about me?"

"Of course I care, goddamnit."

"You're borrowing money to buy food. When is enough enough?" She was sobbing, her mascara running in rivulets down her cheeks.

"Give me some credit. I wouldn't put our lives in jeopardy if I didn't believe that my consulting business was going to be a success. It's growing, Jo. Please be patient. I've got great prospective clients. We're going to make a go of this."

I extended my arms, an invitation for an embrace, and she reluctantly stepped forward. I hugged her, but she was as stiff as a pine board. I couldn't explain to Jo why I couldn't work for other people, because I didn't fully understand why myself.

A month later, in early 1982, one of my former bank clients, Ted Dahlgren, called to ask if I could help him finance some equipment leases with his new company, National Computer Corporation. A former IBM salesman, he was selling used IBM mainframe computers to his former customers at a fraction of the cost of new equipment. IBM only sold new machines, but used equipment was eligible for an IBM service contract, which guaranteed its operation. He was a founder of one of the first companies in the used computer equipment business, International Computer Systems, a third-party leasing company headquartered in Syracuse. They had been one of my customers at BT.

As NCC grew, so, too, did my involvement. I would negotiate the lease contracts with the big company lawyers. At first, they beat me up badly, making it difficult to discount the contracts, but after a few battles, I was able to negotiate the leases to our benefit. Ted was my biggest client, and the only one that paid a monthly retainer.

In early 1983, Ted offered me a job as Chief Financial Officer. My consulting business was going well, but without Ted's retainer, I'd be in trouble. My plan was to grow my business into a statewide consultancy, and the end play was to sell it to a large accounting firm or national business consultancy for a big gain. I was then actively involved in the Syracuse Chamber, and had been elected a member of the Board of Directors and Chairman of the Small Business Council. I had lots of exposure and felt bullish about the future of my business. I kept putting Ted off, concerned that I'd have to give up on my plan, my independence. But worrying about cash flow was stressing my relationship with Jo. I didn't feel like we had a fifty-fifty partnership—I was a risk-taker, she was risk averse. I spent 10 to 12 hours every day working, either with clients or my board relationships. With three young children, we didn't have any social life, because she wouldn't trust anyone with our children. I couldn't afford to take vacations, and even if I could have, I felt the need to be totally immersed in my business, promoting myself, searching for new clients who could keep cash flow going.

Ted offered me a salary of $75,000, significantly more than I was making at the time, almost twice what I had made at my last bank job, but I hesitated. Ted was a likeable guy, but he was all about money. His marriage had broken up years earlier, and he had a severe drinking problem. He got wasted every evening and didn't show up in the office until after 10 the following morning. He'd just be getting warmed up at seven or eight o'clock in the evening, and make you feel like you were slacking off if you went home. Ted was never on time for his appointments, and it was embarrassing. Joint calls were a nightmare, sitting with a banker waiting for Ted to show up. His drinking had cost him his job at ICS—his fellow shareholders couldn't trust him to stay sober. I'd think about his offer, the money and the chance to make a lot more. I wondered if it was all worth it. But I caved. The worry was over. I felt good because now I could focus on doing a job without worrying about where the paycheck was coming from. And Jo would be off my back.

We were a small company and didn't have the equity capital to purchase new equipment and wait two or three years to get our money back. If we couldn't offer our customers lease financing for their new equipment, they'd go somewhere else. It was up to me to find the money to fund these transactions. The answer was wealthy investors.

The tax laws allowed investors to use losses on investments to shelter income. We had to come up with a special leveraged lease tax shelter that offered huge passive losses for investors. I set out to create one of these tax shelters for NCC. It took almost six months to pull all the equipment together for the package. I had numerous meetings with tax attorneys and accountants. I had to become registered with the SEC and pass a Series 63 exam to sell tax-advantaged investments. I hired a securities salesman to canvass small broker-dealers in New York, Connecticut, and Massachusetts, and we went on the road presenting this tax shelter to wealthy investors. It was like going for an IPO, with dog-and-pony shows in multiple cities. We were oversubscribed in our offering, having cleared a profit of over $1 million in the process. Ted threw a company party after the closing, patting me on the back, the glint in his eyes like that of a thief who had just knocked over a Brinks truck.

A $10,000 bonus was enough to put a down payment on our own summer cottage on Sandy Pond. During summers, I commuted from work, about a 45-minute drive. The kids loved the water and I loved spending time with them swimming and fishing and exploring the surrounding territory looking for turtles and frogs.

Soon I was making over $100,000 a year, and totally focused on my business life. Jo took care of everything at home, but she had developed health problems—cardiac arrhythmias—A-fib. Her heart would race double the normal heartbeat; she'd feel anxious and lightheaded with pressure in her chest that felt as if it might explode. I'll never forget the first time it happened in 1974. She was pregnant with Keith and in the middle of the night, she shook me out of a sound sleep.

"Pete … Pete. Something is wrong with me. My heart's racing and I'm having trouble breathing."

Groggy, I rolled over trying to focus on what she had said. She was sitting up in bed, an anxious look on her face.

"What's happening to me? I'm scared."

I checked her pulse and it was fast, around 145 beats per minute. My medical training kicked in.

"Has this ever happened before?"

"No."

"Have you ever been diagnosed with heart problems?"

"Yeah, mitral valve prolapse."

She knew the symptoms as well as I did. Mitral valve prolapse is a weak heart valve, prone to leakage. People with this condition can experience irregular heartbeat, arrhythmia. She had the symptoms of atrial fibrillation, "A-Fib," where the heart valves flutter, failing to close completely, allowing blood to leak, causing the heart to beat faster, making up for loss of blood volume.

"Get dressed. I'm taking you to the ER."

It was about 20 minutes away, and I sped through the little village of Voorheesville to St. Peter's Hospital in Albany as if I were driving an ambulance. I flashed back to all the patients in my dispensary that had needed hospitalization, but as an ethnic minority, Cambodians were seldom welcome in Vietnamese hospitals. Was this payback for not doing enough to help? I imagined Jo throwing a clot, having a stroke, or a brain hemorrhage. I was terrified.

Lying on the gurney in the ER, Jo was frightened. It brought back memories of all the patients I had lost in Vietnam. I remember the faces of gravely wounded Cambodes jabbering in Khmer. I didn't need a translator to understand that they were terrified of dying, and I'd be there when they passed. I had all I could do to keep from panicking.

A-Fib would often convert by itself, but it could take hours for the heart rhythm to normalize. The longer it went on, the higher the risk that the patient could throw a clot, causing a brain hemorrhage, stroke, or worse. I was concerned for Jo's life, and there was nothing I could do except try to keep her calm. Two hours into the event, her heart still racing, the doctors decided to use an antiarrhythmic drug that stops the heart momentarily, causing it to "convert" to a normal rhythm. I held Jo's hand as the drug was injected into her IV, and we waited. She squeezed my hand, her face like one of my Cambodian patients whom I knew would die, and I was frightened. God, please don't take her; please. Ten seconds, 15 seconds, 25, 45, watching the monitor and Jo's erratic heartbeat: please convert, please convert. She was frightened. I thought about our unborn child, what would happen to him? I held my breath, counting the seconds. At 60 seconds, her heart rate dropped and within seconds was within normal range. The chest pain and anxious feeling subsided. I could see relief in Jo's face, and I thanked God for sparing Jo and our child.

It happened a second time in 1983, the year I joined NCC. My secretary interrupted me in a contract negotiation, with the message that Jo was having an A-Fib attack. I was annoyed. I told the secretary to ask Matt to meet her at the ER. Two hours later, Jo called to let me know that she was all right. I realized then how far our relationship had deteriorated when I heard her voice. I felt guilty and selfish. I thought about how hardened I had become, how ruthless, another Ted focused solely on making money. To hell with loved ones. To hell with weak people. To hell with needy people.

Meanwhile, I fed my need for risk-taking. I was into fast boats. Starting out with a used 18-foot boat powered by a modified 200-horsepower outboard motor, I'd scream up and down the Pond shoreline until I blew the engine. The next boat was a 21-foot inboard with a Chevy 350 V8 engine. It was fast for a while, but soon got boring. I needed something that would bring me to the edge. I found it in a 30-foot offshore race boat with twin big-block Chevy engines that put out over 700 horses. This was a boat that I could jump the massive waves on Lake Ontario during storms. The fun lasted for a couple of years until I had an accident that caused me to bite off my lower lip, requiring plastic surgery. Had I not been drinking, it probably wouldn't have happened.

Jo's 40th birthday was a cause for celebration. We had a huge party up at the Pond and invited all of our friends. I bought her a 1986 Corvette for her birthday. She was thrilled, but so was I. On my trips back and forth between Syracuse and the Pond during summers, I would routinely borrow her car. It was so easy to push the Vette over 100 mph on I-81. My mind would wander back to the days when I'd parachute over majestic forests, pastures, and streams that glistened in the sunlight.

In the spring of 1985 with the success of our first leveraged lease investment package, we decided to ramp up our securities department and develop more shelters. I hired two more salesmen with experience selling wholesale investment products to regional broker-dealers, and a securities lawyer, as well as several support personnel, including one responsible for discounting lease transactions. Over the course of the next 18 months, we sold three more tax shelters. I was busy traveling, calling on regional broker-dealers. When back in Syracuse, I pushed NCC salesmen to originate more lease transactions, and arranged larger lines of credit from my banker friends to warehouse these leases in preparation for packaging them into shelters.

In late 1986, tax law reform swept through Washington. The Tax Reform Act, signed into law in October, closed the loopholes in the tax code that we had relied on to raise money, putting an end to tax shelters as we knew them. In anticipation of this change, I developed relationships with large leasing companies that bought our leases, but at a reduced profit margin. We had to cut expenses drastically. We had grown to a company with 56 people and needed to cut overhead. We laid off 30 people company-wide, 10 in my department, dismantling our entire broker-dealer operation. Salesmen were the last to lose their jobs, because according to Ted, without sales, there is no business. He had no use for support personnel. We were a necessary evil, and I was one of them.

We had over $20 million in warehouse lines of credit at three banks, and the banks were nervous. They demanded cash flow reports from us, and I met with them weekly to review our progress. I know now that if I had not been at NCC, the banks would have closed us down. They trusted me as one of them. We pulled out of our tailspin by the third quarter of 1987, and generated a profit for the year. Business in 1988 and 1989 was strong. Our profit soared, and so, too, did my earnings. I was grossing over a $175,000 a year. Jo and I were finally comfortable financially. We bought a new summer home on Wellesley Island in the St. Lawrence River, and a big cabin cruiser. I drove a new Mercedes and spent money like there was no limit to income. I could see myself easily making $500,000 a year. Hell, some of our salesmen were already there; the top guy was making close to a million. My monthly nut was over $12,500 and growing, between mortgage payments and taxes, auto and boat loans, and credit cards, and I saw no downside in sight.

I traveled frequently on business during this time, building and maintaining relationships with large leasing companies, corporate and institutional investors, and attending leasing trade group meetings, often held in warm and exotic locations—Palm Springs, Nassau, Bermuda, and Acapulco. I'd walk resort campuses and beaches, wishing that Jo was with me, trying to rekindle the relationship we had before our marriage. Maybe it was a trust issue with her, too. I don't know. She especially didn't want my parents' help. Jo was an obsessive cleaner, and my mother was just the opposite: dishes in the sink, bed unmade, etc. My parents weren't good enough for Jo. It stretched my relationship with them to the limit, and at times, I'm sorry to say, I agreed with Jo. I looked down on them. I knew my relationship with Jo was in trouble. She struggled with her weight, yo-yoing 30 or 40 pounds in a year. I tried to be supportive, but there wasn't much I said that worked. I was just the opposite, going to the gym obsessively every morning.

TED HIRED SEVERAL SALESMEN in 1990 from his former company, ICS, which had gone bankrupt a year earlier. These guys were the cream of the crop, as far as he was concerned. We guaranteed one of them a $500,000 draw. As the year went on, it became apparent that we had made a mistake bringing them onboard. Their sales numbers were way off budget, and we needed to do something about it. Ted was reluctant to let them go, and he wanted to fire support staff. He didn't understand what we did behind the scenes, and I was to blame because I made it look so easy. I offered to leave the company, since I was the highest paid support person. It took him by surprise.

I sat across from his desk as he stared off into space, then he snapped out of it.

"I know we need to do something, but I don't want to let you go. You're an important part of this company."

I was glad to hear this. My offer was a gamble, but I couldn't afford to leave with no comparable job in sight. I had interviewed with two big leasing companies after Ted had hired all those ICS guys. The bigger problem was that the new people were poisoning NCC's culture and our company was suffering. I gave Ted an ultimatum:

"Make me the Chief Operating Officer. Let's dig into the numbers and decide where we need to cut."

He looked relieved, as if I had given him a way out of our standoff. In difficult negotiating situations, Ted was a master salesman and good at disguising his true feelings. He looked upbeat and confident.

"I like your idea. What if I promote you to Executive Vice President and COO; how's that?"

He knocked me off my feet. Did he really do that: give me the authority to make personnel decisions? Now I can exert some influence, some control over Ted's spending on people who couldn't help us. We shook hands. I walked out of his office and called Jo to tell her that Ted finally decided to trust me to do the right thing at the company.

However, Ted also promoted one of the salesmen, Ron Volk, to sales manager, and he began tightening up on the salesmen. Ron had designs on the EVP job, and wasn't too happy when I got it. Tension was palpable. I ran weekly staff meetings to review departmental progress goals. Ted never attended any of the meetings, and Ron begrudgingly paid me lip service. The meetings went on for several months, but nothing ever came of my recommendations. I began to think that Ted had promoted me to shut me up. I had no operational authority. Ted still made all the decisions. I should have known he'd never change. I felt used, trapped. I couldn't afford to leave NCC and had no employment offers in sight. I needed to get out of there.

I began working on a backup plan. I had come up with a leasing structure that could help big banks increase their capital base. I broached the subject with Ted and he was excited. We were talking about huge deals, in the hundreds of millions, and his face lit up. I opened a branch office in Madison, New Jersey, a short distance from Manhattan and the headquarters for most of the big banks. I spent a year working out of that office. Ted was out of my face, and I had hopes that any payoff would lead to my financial freedom. I could take the money and leave NCC.

I developed a sale-leaseback product that involved NCC buying all of a bank's assets that didn't make them any money, like buildings, furniture, automobiles, and corporate jets, and leasing it all back to them. With our cash, the bank could invest in mortgages and commercial loans that generate income. The structure would have an immediate positive impact on their capital ratio and improve bank profitability.

While I was off making calls to the major banks in Manhattan, Ted hired a weasel from ICS with the nickname "Teflon John," to be our new CFO. He sorted through our expenses and presented a list of people who could be cut, all staff positions. Three weeks later, I was on the phone with the Syracuse office and got the news on a late Friday afternoon before I drove home for the weekend—Matt had been fired. I would never have fired him. He was knowledgeable and good at what he did. I was still the EVP/COO and angry about not being notified, but that didn't matter to Ted. He was going to do whatever he wanted, just as he always had. A week later, Ted announced that everyone in the company would take a pay cut, and there would be no more bonuses. My pay was cut to $75,000. I was in trouble, and told Ted I couldn't live on that. I began to curse the day that I had ever joined him, but now, I had him where I wanted him. The deals I was working on totaled over $750 million. Even if only one of them came through, it would pull the company out of the woods. He was enthralled, and he agreed to lend me $4,500 per month to cover my bills.

IT WAS A DIFFICULT TIME in our marriage. I had kept Jo informed all along, and we both hoped that the deals I was working on in New York City would set me free. Jo was edgy, because I was edgy. She knew all about Ted, his alcoholism, phone calls at 2:00 a.m., his obsession with making money, and she could see that I had fallen for his sales pitch. I wasn't happy; I felt like a shackled prisoner. I had gotten myself into a position where I had no options available. I was too far in hock to walk away, and when I told her about Matt and the salary cut, she lost it.

"How could you do this to us? You've led us out on the financial cliff."

Her face was tomato red, her saliva spraying all over me as her words hit me in the solar plexus.

"You didn't seem to mind our summer home, the Corvette, the boat."

I caught her off-balance.

"I wanted us to become financially solvent. I truly believed that we could do it. I thought I could deal with Ted, to manage him, but he got the best of me. I bought his program. I'm trapped. I can't stand him. He cares for no one. All he wants is money. That's not me, but it's too late."

Standing in front of Jo, I felt an overwhelming surge of emotion and started crying. I felt sick to my stomach. At least a minute went by while Jo watched me sob. I looked at her and said I'm sorry.

"What are you going to do?" she said in a calm and deliberate voice.

"What can I do? I'm stuck right now. I have to stay with him for the time being while I figure out my next move." Jo raised her arms.

"Then we need to put Wellesley Island up for sale. The boat, too."

Every Friday afternoon on my drive from New Jersey back to Syracuse, I'd call Ted and spend an hour giving him a report about our progress. It was exciting, the thought of putting such big deals together. We had three large banks that were very interested in the package, but the lease structure was controversial, and a tough sell with conservative institutional lenders. Not surprisingly, it was the weaker banks that were most interested. Unfortunately, they were difficult to finance, and I couldn't find lenders willing to take the risk. Our plan was not working.

I knew the road was coming to a dead end in the spring of 1991. I continued talking up the program with Ted, knowing that if he saw the effort as fruitless, he'd stop lending me money. I made plans to go back into consulting, and lined up a few clients beforehand. The economy was again in a slump, and it was during these times that my consulting business was strongest. Customers were getting kicked out of the banks again, and I still had good relationships with asset-based lenders. In May 1991, I tendered my resignation.

Bob M

I was consumed with questions about my experience in Nam and my life since, especially the moral issues, but there were few answers. I just couldn't get at the details, and I wasn't sure I wanted to know. My subconscious had done a laudable job of protecting me from myself, but had nevertheless influenced my conscious thoughts and actions. I couldn't hide visceral reactions and didn't know why. I had discovered a spiritual life in prayer, which gave me respite but no answers. I felt an emptiness that I couldn't explain or reconcile. I thought reconnecting with my Special Forces roots would help. I called a medic buddy of mine in 1990 and asked him if he was interested in going to the Special Forces Association annual meeting in DC that year. He was game.

Bob McCann had been my best friend in Training Group, and had come home with me a couple of weekends from Fort Bragg. My family really liked him, too. He even dated Alice. I ran into him several times during my tour. He was the medic at the A-Camp where I got hit. He saw me come in with the Mike Force and I think he was jealous of all the action I saw. Frankly I would have traded places with him in an instant. By then, I had seen enough war for a lifetime. I went out to LA to visit with him after getting out of the service. He was a student at UC Long Beach and was sharing an apartment with a cop. He opened the door and a rush of bluish smoke almost knocked me over. He passed a joint. I took a hit and sat in a chair facing his recliner. The living room was a combination of Salvation Army furniture and military detritus. A camo poncho liner covered his recliner. There were pictures of Nam everywhere.

On a side table next to an ashtray was a half-size human head that almost looked fake, like the rubber shrunken heads you can buy at the mall. It was the color of dark chocolate with long black hair covering most of the skull, its lips sewn shut with coarse thread. The nose was large, dwarfing its face. Next to it were a string of ears and several fingers, also blackish and shriveled, less than human size. I asked him where he got the souvenirs and he said it was the head of an NVA soldier. The fingers and ears were from other corpses. An old Cambode had shown him how to preserve the flesh. How he smuggled it out of country I don't know. Bob smirked, and jokingly said that the collection of body parts was what he had to show for his efforts in Nam. I had trouble understanding where he was coming from; he wasn't the same guy I knew in Training Group.

"Bunard, remember? You guys had come up from Long Hái to run some ops along the road to Cambodia. I was the fucking camp medic."

"What, too boring for you?"

"Ah, the camp routines drove me nuts. I wanted to be on the Mike Force and see some action."

"Yeah. You could have been in that firefight with me and we could have ridden McGuire rigs together to the MASH."

"Fuck you, man; you know what I mean. I remember that day, seeing that chopper drag you and the other guy out. That must have been some ride."

"I thought it was my last."

"After that operation, I volunteered for Special Operations."

"Did the change agree with you?"

"For a while it did. There were some crazy motherfuckers on that team. We'd go out on three and four man recon teams for days at a time. I got my fill of excitement plus."

"What do you mean?"

"Some of those guys took stupid chances, like playing roulette. We were on an operation in Cambodia, about 25 klicks over the border, searching for the headquarters of the Fifth NVA Division. You know the drill. No air support, no artillery, no nothing. We were totally on our own, like how Charlie feels when he's snooping around our backyard in South Vietnam. Talk about the tables being turned. It scared the shit out of me. It took us six days to cover the distance on foot; we humped. We began running into training patrols at night. You couldn't get much sleep, because you had to be ready to move out. It was nerve wracking. We found the outer perimeter on day six. Then we reconned the area."

"Yeah, so what did you find?"

"It was a division-size base camp, sure enough, with a sophisticated perimeter system, bunkers, and machine gun emplacements. During the evenings, we snuck beyond the perimeter to get a closer look at the base infrastructure. It was well developed. There were many permanent buildings, gravel roads, artillery, hundreds of tanks, trucks, and other military vehicles. Shit, I thought I was back at Bragg.

"After three days, we felt we had gathered enough intelligence to head back across the border. Under cover of darkness, we passed through the perimeter at the south end of the base. As we crawled under the concertina wire, there was a guard taking a piss not 10 meters away, whistling and paying more attention to his dick than what was going on around him. We could have waited until he had finished and gone back to his bunker, but our asshole first lieutenant decided to put him out of his misery. He crawled toward the guard, figuring he'd sneak up behind him and slit his throat, but when he was halfway there, the guard heard the rustling in the leaves and spun around with his AK to his shoulder, screaming, "ai đi ở đợ, ai đi ở đợ, ai đi ở đợ?"

"What happened, Bob?"

"It was like slow motion, man; the guard kept yelling. He couldn't see us and we didn't know whether he was going to spray us with live-fire, or give up on the notion that someone or something was out there. Then the lieutenant, our CO, bolted upright, aimed and fired his pistol at point-blank range and the guard collapsed in a heap. He ran over, took out his knife and cut off the guard's left ear, while he lay on the ground screaming.

"What the fuck did he do that for?"

"He was green. This was his first mission. The other guy on our team, a master sergeant, said the same thing, but didn't have time to elaborate. We jumped up and hightailed it into the jungle. It would only be a matter of time before they mustered up a search party to look for us. There were training operations all over the territory between there and the Ho Chi Minh Trail. We didn't know whether they had commo. If they did, we were fucked."

"Did they ever come after you?"

"Oh yeah, it didn't take long for them to pull a couple of platoons of Regulars together. They pressed us hard. We had to keep moving, mostly at night. We hid during the day, but we couldn't sleep. We were exhausted. One afternoon, I think it was three days into our exit plan, we were hiding in some really thick shit on the side of a hill. We could see them coming right toward us. The three of us split up and I hid myself under jungle growth next to a giant tree. I could hear their boots crushing the undergrowth right next to my head as they passed by, one after another. I know if they had found me, they would have dragged my ass back to their base and paraded me through the local villages in a cage. Or maybe they'd just slit my throat right then and there in retribution for killing one of their own, just like we would have done.

"I lay there with red ants crawling over my face and down my fatigue shirt biting me. After the boots went away, I tore my shirt off and hundreds of ants fell away. I brushed off the rest, leaving tons of little red bites.

"We decided to lay low until dusk, and head out due south. We walked until daybreak, and climbed a mountain to get a better idea of our location. The terrain was difficult, and the hill had caves, some of which had been used by Cambodians trying to defend their territory against the NVA. We reached the top of the mountain and glassed the surrounding area. We could see several villages in the distance and one in particular, the village just across the border from Katum. It was probably six klicks from the mountain, and it was on the Cambodian side of the Ho Chi Minh Trail. There were cooking fires all along the horizon looking toward the border. Some of them were probably safe areas off the Trail where the NVA hid during daylight. We decided to make our way toward the Trail, but wait to cross until darkness, when the safe areas would be empty. We hiked all day and stopped about a klick from the Trail to wait for darkness. The lieutenant wanted to set up an ambush, but Turner, the master sergeant, had had enough of the lieutenant's grandstanding. It went like this:

'Lieutenant, we're crossing the Trail and making way for Katum, as per the original plan.'

'Sergeant, what if I told you that I was giving you an order?'

'Go right ahead, sir.'

'You know, sergeant, I could have you court-marshaled for refusing to take a direct order.'

'That's right, sir. You could just do that after we get back to base. But that's a long way off. A lot can happen between now and then.'

'Sergeant, are you threatening me?'

'No, sir, but as the story goes, you could have been killed back there at the perimeter. Or, would you rather me tell Colonel Miller about your lapse in judgment?'

The lieutenant was furious, but we didn't set up an ambush that night. We crossed the trail without incident, and were in the Katum team house sipping Jim Beam the next evening.

'So what happened to the lieutenant?'

"Well, he got a Bronze Star for bravery under hostile conditions, but the pact between Turner and him was never broken. The lieutenant got what he wanted, and so did Turner and I. That's when I decided I'd had enough of Special Ops. Shit, two weeks before the end of my tour, they wanted me to go on another mission with the lieutenant. I refused. He threatened me with a court-martial, but somehow that threat never went anywhere. I ETS'd and haven't heard jack since."

"Your lieutenant sounds like the asshole captain that got me shot. He was the other guy swinging from that chopper."

After talking with Bob, I decided to go through the hundreds of slides I had taken in Vietnam. I had 50 pictures printed in preparation for the SFA meeting, expecting to have a good laugh with other former Green Beanies, but as the time approached for the meeting, I lost interest in chest pounding about Nam and reviling our Vietnamese enemy. I never went.

Bob was promoted to Assistant General Manager at the National Brewery near Syracuse in 1985. He spent three years in the area, but we didn't talk much. He and his family came up to visit us for a day at our summer camp on Sandy Pond. It was the first time I had met his wife and two kids. We had a pleasant day, but Bob seemed remote, like he was somewhere else. Several years later, Jo got a call from Sandy, Bob's wife. She said that Bob had walked out on her and the kids unannounced. Jo looked at me, wondering if I knew what was going on. I hadn't talked with Bob since their visit, but I sensed that maybe he was dealing with demons from Nam. Later, he told me that he had just gotten tired of Sandy and the kids; they were getting on his nerves.

Bob never talked about his feelings and I was beginning to think that there might be more to my own confused state of mind than I realized.

Financial Storm

I was drowning in a sea of debt. The first year back in the consulting business went well enough, but I couldn't pay all my bills. Without Ted's monthly loan, I fell behind on everything but my mortgages. The summer home and the cabin cruiser went on the block. The monthly payment between those two was about $4,500. I scrambled to put them on the market. The house was listed for $325,000 in late May, $10,000 less than I had invested. The real estate market was stagnant, and the selling season short, from April to September. The summer dragged on as people strolled around the property, sightseers curious about how the rich people live. I felt anything but rich. I was a fool, allowing myself to be taken in by Ted's blurred vision of what was important in life. I should have listened to my gut. In August, I dropped the price on the house to $310,000, but that only encouraged the bottom feeders, who low-balled me with offers only desperate people would accept. Ironically, had I been in their shoes, I would have tried to horse-trade myself.

The market for used boats was even softer than real estate. I owed $115,000 on the boat, and listings in national boating publications were running between $45,000 and $75,000. I had fallen behind on my Mercedes. I owed a bank $50,000 for repair work on the boathouse at Wellesley, and $54,000 to Ted. I had $40,000 in credit card debt. My monthly debt payments were $12,500 with only $5,000 in monthly income.

It was easy to present a positive attitude with consulting clients struggling with cash flow because I knew firsthand how difficult and demoralizing it was. I knew how to borrow money, and the bankers trusted me. My presentation memoranda used the same format that lending officers and credit analysts used to approve loans, so I did the banker's work for them. They knew they couldn't bullshit me. I was one of them, but I wasn't. None of the bankers I did business with knew anything about my credit problems.

The summer home sold the week before Labor Day for $286,000. I lost all my equity, but was able to pay off the $50,000 boathouse loan. I sold the boat that same weekend for $77,500 and convinced the bank to write off the remaining balance of $37,500. Over the next two years, I returned the Mercedes to the dealer and negotiated with the three largest credit cards to settle for 10 cents on the dollar. Two of the credit cards would not negotiate with me.

I began thinking that bankruptcy might be the only way to clear the slate, but I was reluctant, feeling a moral obligation to pay something, pay what I could afford. I hired a bankruptcy attorney and he drafted a letter for the credit card lenders asking them to settle with me, telling them that they would at least get something versus zero from the bankruptcy court. They refused.

At dinner one evening in late April, Rich and Ben were at the table with us and the chatter was all about them. Rich was a sophomore in high school and Ben was in middle school. Keith was off at college. Jo and I didn't exchange words until both the boys left the table to do their homework. She cleared the table without as much as a glance at me.

"I thought I had the credit card lenders willing to accept a haircut, but now they're both refusing. I told them if they didn't, I was going to declare bankruptcy."

Jo was loading the dishwasher and didn't respond.

"What do you think, Jo?"

She put down a dish and looked at me, anger written all over her face.

"About what? Bankruptcy, our financial situation, the incessant collection calls."

I stood up from the table and walked over to the sink where she was standing.

"About the three-year struggle to clear my debts without declaring bankruptcy, about trying to do the right thing."

"The right thing for who—you?"

"Come on. I'm doing the best I can do under the circumstances. I can't force the credit card people to accept my offer. And if they don't, all the other deals I've negotiated will fall through."

"You and your deals. I hate you. I don't care what you do," and she stormed out of the kitchen.

I was tired of three years of collection calls, tired of endless conversations with lenders. I tossed in the towel and filed for bankruptcy in May of 1994, three years to the month from leaving NCC. Jo was not included in the bankruptcy filing.

I left my attorney's office feeling the way I had when I was fired from the bank. There was an empty feeling in my gut. I had often denigrated people who filed for bankruptcy, thinking of them as losers. Now I was the loser. I had no money, my consulting business was bumbling along, and my wife felt as if I had forsaken her. We had no financial stability; I had long since cashed in what little retirement account I had. My debts were wiped clean, the slate cleared, but at great personal cost. I no longer had a stellar credit rating, something that I had carefully cultivated for years.

Jo couldn't understand why I couldn't have stuck it out with NCC, like other people do, why I had compromised our financial health by borrowing so much money. Shortly after leaving NCC, she decided to go back to work, but had no interest in nursing. She enrolled in a medical records curriculum at the community college, and just before I declared bankruptcy, she got a job in the medical records department at St. Mary's Hospital. We needed to gain some financial stability in our life, and I decided that I would seek to merge my consulting practice with a regional Certified Public Accounting firm. I identified several possibilities, and Brown Alden & Company was the best fit with five offices across upstate New York. I met with the partners and presented a proposal to bring investment banking and financial services to their clients. The meeting went well, and in August, we merged.

I opened a Syracuse office for them and began introducing my clients. I had a few deals in the pipeline, which came to fruition over the next year. I helped a few of their clients refinance loans, but some of the partners were reluctant to share their clients with me. It meant sharing their income. There was acrimony over the managing partner's growth plans. He had expanded the firm into nontraditional areas that the other more conservative partners thought diluted the firm's resources. They were unhappy with our association, because they had to share profits with me. After three-and-a-half years with the firm, I could see that the managing partner was under pressure to get rid of me. I negotiated a fee sharing arrangement with clients I had brought to the firm and we split in March of 1998.

Jo didn't take the news well. We were having dinner out just before the split.

"I'm leaving Brown Alden. The love affair is over. Some of the partners are upset with the merger. They want to unwind it."

"Why?"

"They don't want to share profits with me. They don't want to introduce me to their clients. They're provincial, myopic, and opinionated, they don't like me, and I don't trust them."

"What are you going to do, get another job?"

"No. I'm really finished this time. I can't work for anyone else. I'm going back into consulting."

Her facial expression said it all.

"Here we go with the trust thing. You're 53, have no steady income, and no retirement. How could you do this to me?"

"Honey, I'm sorry. I can't work for someone else. Think of it this way. The most I ever made with the accounting firm was $60,000 a year. I'll match that in my consulting business. You're working. We'll be fine."

She shut down and we finished the meal in silence.

The Split

I'll never forget how Jo dropped the bomb. We had just finished a colossal garage sale liquidating a lifetime collection of antiques. Even after our home was filled with furniture, I continued searching for that special piece. I found curious satisfaction in breathing life into the derelict possessions of others. Over the 28 years of our marriage, my obsession filled a home, a summer cottage, and a two-story, two-car garage. Every spring, we talked about having a garage sale to make room for our cars, but never did. A few weeks after I split from Brown Allen, Jo insisted that we get rid of things we weren't using—everything in the garage.

Organizing the sale was a huge undertaking, sorting and pricing a mountain of antiques. As I pulled furniture out of the loft, the memories of each piece sprang to life. I wondered about the families who had owned this or that object, once cherished, now marred by neglect. I had pulled the Lincoln rocker from a burn pile; its curvaceous walnut arms mimicked a swan's neck. I remembered how the wood felt in my hands, its texture rough, bereft of moisture and black with weather, the cane seat destroyed. Now it was a work of art, beautiful yet functional. We had rocked our babies to sleep in that chair. The beautiful Hoosier with stained glass windows and a flower mill, which had been home to generations of barn swallows, I restored for our summer home on Wellesley Island. The oak press-back cane seat chairs from our cottage on Sandy Pond had been covered in layers of nondescript depression-era paint, their legs broken and seat bottoms missing; now they were restored to their original condition and natural grain, and were alluring in their design and utility. My collection choked our longish driveway before we had emptied the garage.

We held the sale over a three-day weekend. It was exhausting. On the last day, Jo practically gave things away; she seemed driven to get rid of everything, almost frantic. I didn't object; it was cathartic in a way, but I had an unsettled feeling in the pit of my stomach. As I watched my treasures disappear at the end of the driveway, I wondered how one measures the worth of a man's labor. The sale only netted $3,200.

As I counted the cash, Jo thrust her hand out without a word, and demanded a split. I looked at her, taken aback by her assertiveness. I hesitated for a moment in search of rationale for behavior that was familiar yet unfamiliar, and without a word, handed over half the take.

I thought we had a good working relationship, the two of us, but she had difficulty expressing her feelings. I was the emotional one in the relationship, always the one to apologize, even if I wasn't wholly at fault. She was good at building walls; I had always been good at climbing them. I should have seen it coming. I could tell things finally changed between us when I had told her four months earlier that I was quitting my corporate job, the fifth in the 25 years since college. It was the familiar cycle: get fired or escape, become a consultant and grovel for cash flow, and when we were broke, get back on the gerbil wheel. But this time, the cycle had to stop, I told her. I would no longer work for men I could neither trust nor respect. When challenged by a perfidious manager, I withdrew and became depressed. When they pushed me, we'd have confrontations. I couldn't trust myself and had to get away. Only one time did I lose control, and thankfully, one of my coworkers was there to stop me. I couldn't rationalize my behavior and was afraid to talk with Jo about it for fear that she'd have thought I was crazy. When I finally quit, I felt her wall go up. Whenever she got like this, I would ask what bothered her and try to coax an answer. This time, there was no answer. Even so, I never considered that our marriage was at risk.

She folded the money quickly and stuffed it into her jeans pocket, then looked up at me, and nervously delivered her lines as if rehearsed.

"I'm leaving you. We're going in different directions. You have your business and I need some time by myself."

I looked at her in disbelief. For a few seconds, I tried to put the words in context, but couldn't. I was in shock. I could feel my face flush; the nerves in my spine tingled and my head felt like it was going to burst.

I blurted "Don't you want to go to counseling?"

Tears had formed in the corners of her eyes and were streaming down her cheeks. Hesitating for a few seconds, she started with her hands and arms.

"I've already gone to counseling and it won't work."

I could see that she was visibly anxious, almost apologetic but determined, a familiar trait: she would anticipate me questioning her motives and have a ready-made answer, but I could always turn her around. This time was different. I could feel the sudden shock of abandonment, as it swept through my body, drowning every cell, every molecule like a tidal wave. Then my body shuddered and I gave it up. As I stood there sobbing uncontrollably, I begged her not to break up our family.

"But why don't you want to go to counseling with me?"

Almost pleading, she said, "That's not the answer, Pete. I'm sorry, but I need to be by myself."

"What does 'I need to be by myself' mean? Do you want a divorce?"

She slowly wiped tears from her face, as if searching for an answer.

"I don't know."

"Then we've got a chance?"

"Yeah … maybe."

I didn't believe her. I knew her too well. Our marriage was over, just like that. I would never have divorced her, never have left her. I had promised her a lifetime of devotion. I had even given my word to her father on his deathbed. I felt an obligation to protect her, to stay with her: me, the loyalist, never-give-up, stick-with-it-until-it-hurts guy. I felt betrayed, alone. I shivered as my tears turned cold.

The next few hours were a blur. No one else was at home. I sat on the couch wondering what had happened. It was a nightmare. It was reality. Then I thought about my sons and what I would tell them. I wanted so much to push the blame on their mother. I looked around the sitting room. Jo was everywhere I looked—the wing-back chair, Queen Anne loveseat, the framed needlework over the Tam o' Shanter lampshade—Home Sweet Home. What had I done?

RICH AND BEN TOOK IT HARDEST. They sat on the couch in the family room while I broke the news.

"Your mother and I have decided to separate. She left this evening."

They sat together, staring blankly at the family room floor trying to process what I had said. It was as if I had detonated a bomb in front of them. They were catatonic. Ben, 16, didn't ask any questions; he just looked up at me with the look of a child who had been told his parents were dead, and started crying.

"Your mother and I are going in different directions, and we need some time to ourselves," I said.

Rich, 21 and a college student, just sat silently, trying to absorb the news.

"Are you going to get divorced?" asked Ben.

"I don't know, honey; I hope not," I said, knowing well enough that there was no hope of reconciliation. Jo had carefully left the door open when I asked her point blank, but she patronized me.

Ben continued to sob. Rich looked up at me, his eyes red and moist, weeping.

"Dad, this sucks. Can't you two go to counseling?"

"Honey, we're still talking. There's a chance that we can save the marriage."

Later that evening, I fed Keith the same line of bullshit when he came home from work. I knew it wasn't the truth. I knew there was no hope. It wasn't a mutual decision. Why did I lie to my sons? I would have told them the truth, had I known it then. Jo had absolutely no security; we had no savings after my bankruptcy. She had ridden the roller coaster as far as she could.

The months after our separation were traumatic. I was depressed, and constant feelings of guilt never let up. I dove into my work. Consulting clients carried me through those few months of lawyers arguing to settle what Jo and I had already agreed to—yet she hired a piranha because she didn't trust me. A year to the day of our separation agreement, the divorce became final in the fall of 1998. All through this ordeal, I tried to maintain regular contact with my sons, holding weekly dinners for them and the grandkids at my new home. I never denigrated their mother, or blamed her for our breakup. I trusted that she wasn't badmouthing me, but it felt like this giant wedge had been driven between my sons and me, and it hurt deeply.

PART III

COMING TO TERMS

Cape Cod

Renee and I were on our third trip to Cape Cod in as many months, her mother an emotional shipwreck following her father's death. It was Memorial Day weekend, 2005, and during these visits, we would often slip away to one of the Cape's many wonderful diversions. Chatham had always held special significance for me, a place where my children spent summers on the beach. Our family wiled away countless hours traipsing up and down side streets not frequented by tourists. I have found special comfort in those memories in the years since Jo and I divorced.

I remember the first time I met Renee, at a Chamber of Commerce networking event in 1986. She was a Chamber employee staffing the booth, and a buddy of mine introduced us. She was intellectual, confident, professional, and gorgeous: about five-eight, auburn hair to her shoulders, clear skin with a hint of freckles, brown eyes, and a great figure. Jo and I had been married for 17 years at that time, and while we had our issues, I wasn't a philanderer. Still, I could see myself with Renee. The next time I saw Renee was at a business seminar in 1998. Jo had filed for divorce, and after months of depression, I had begun dating.

Warmed by the afternoon sun, Renee and I strolled around the provincial little village of Chatham. The streets were busy with townies and tourists, difficult to tell apart except for the manner of dress or the presence of shopping bags. Shops catering to eclectic tastes were peppered among those that sold T-shirts and suntan lotion. Tourists vied for parking spaces on the street, shoe-horning their BMWs and Mercedes in between the townies' pickup trucks and Jeeps.

As we were about to enter one of those interesting little gift shops on the main street, my cell phone rang. It was an appendage on the side of my hip even on vacation, the reality of counseling small business clients in an emergency always a possibility.

"Are you Peter McShane, the Green Beret Medic?" the caller asked.

I affirmed it unwittingly, before I had time to think about the string of words ringing in my ear. It was Ronald Stoddard, a medic classmate from Special Forces training. The son of a genteel southern businessman, Ronald was a smooth talker; his easy southern drawl could lull one to sleep.

"Hey, thanks for taking my call. I wasn't sure if you wanted to talk to me. I still remember you, pale-faced and hungover, standing in the back of formation one morning down at Fort Sam, flipping me the bird, and Sergeant Madison dropping you for pushups."

He chuckled as he finished the sentence. I had received a voice mail from him a few days earlier about a reunion, and frankly wasn't interested. My memories from Special Forces were safely tucked away, and I did everything to avoid thinking about that time in my life.

"What's up, Ronald?"

"Me and David Condon—you remember David—we thought it would be good to get a bunch of us together for a reunion. What you been doin' for the last 36 years?"

I really didn't want to talk about it, but now I felt compelled to at least give him an answer without going into any detail.

"Got married, went back to college, got a job, had three kids, had a few more jobs, got divorced, got remarried, and that brings us to today."

There was silence for more than a few seconds. I thought we might have lost the connection.

"Yeah, sounds familiar. I traveled around the country with David for a while; really never have had a steady job. I got married, but couldn't settle down. I had a lot of trouble with relationships. I've got PTSD. I'm counseling vets now."

I thought it was all bullshit; Ronald was always all about himself. Standing in a sea of people on the curb outside the gift shop, I was trying to put Ronald's words into perspective, and felt self-conscious, like people were listening to what he was saying. Perspiration soaked my underarms. I told him I'd think about the reunion, just to get him off the phone.

Renee had long since gone into the shop, and was coming out as I tried to resurrect my memory of Ronald. There were a thousand stories, most with him at the center. What came to mind was a debriefing before formation one early Monday morning, about his weekend in Savannah with a sweet young lady who had delighted him with her familiarity of his erogenous zones. As he described how she kissed his nipples and then flicked the ends with her tongue, the first sergeant yelled "FALL IN!"

Renee had run into her mother's neighbor in the gift shop and they were having a conversation about shopping, the weather, and the never-ending traffic on the Cape during tourist season. I could hear them speak, but I was suspended somewhere between past and present, not a participant in their conversation. Lost in the recesses of my mind, I tried to carefully dissect what Ronald had said, without unnecessarily disturbing memories deeply buried.

"Who was that on the phone?" she asked.

"It was a friend from Special Forces. He wanted to know if I would be interested in going to a reunion in September."

She was surprised. In the seven years we had been together, I had avoided talk about my time in the military.

"Wow … are you going?"

"I don't know. I need to think about it," I said defensively.

It was four thirty and Chatham's streets were clearing as the dinner hour approached. Her mother's neighbor bid farewell, leaving Renee and me a moment to ourselves. I reached for her hand as we walked toward the car. We glanced at one another, smiled, and I remembered our first date. A few days after we met at the seminar, I asked her to lunch. It was a busy downtown restaurant and as we talked, I could feel energy, a connection. It was so easy and comfortable I don't even remember the words we spoke. Sincere and self-deprecating, she disarmed me. I can remember leaving the restaurant that afternoon, oblivious to the lunch-hour rush around us, and when she turned to say goodbye, I leaned in close and kissed her gently on the lips. It was simply sensational. The following weekend we went to the downtown jazz fest, and bathed in each other's essence. We danced in the street that Saturday afternoon, the music bringing us together in body and soul. Our spiritual connection was stronger than I had ever experienced. We married in June of 2001.

That evening after dinner, Renee and I took a walk on the beach near her mother's home. It was near sunset, deserted. We walked to the waters' edge and sat down side by side with our feet in the water. I put my arm around her and pulled her close. The slow, metronomic rhythm of the evening surf caressing the sand was comforting, peaceful, ethereal. The pinks, blues, and grays of the sunset framed the horizon, the water tracing its image for as far as one could see, but my mind roiled.

"You look like you're deep in thought." She turned to look at me. "You haven't said a word all evening."

"It's Ronald's conversation, I mean what he told me. He's a storyteller, all right, but how do you make up shit like that?" Renee was surprised by my intensity.

"What do you mean?"

"Ronald said he struggled with drugs and alcohol, couldn't hold a job, blew up his marriage, and suffered a nervous breakdown. Of all people, if you asked me who in our class could have had a nervous breakdown, it wouldn't have been Ronald. He was as cool as a block of ice."

Renee reached for my hand and held it tenderly.

"Honey, you don't know what's happened in his life; but for the grace of God it may have been you."

"I'm sorry, I just can't believe him. I mean, Khe Sanh was a bad scene, but Ronald was never wounded. So how come I haven't had a nervous breakdown?"

"There must be a lot more to his story than you know."

"Oh, knowing him, I'm sure there is but I don't want to hear it."

I woke up before dawn with a nightmare, my pajamas saturated in perspiration. I couldn't remember specifics, but it was Nam, I was running from the NVA, and they were about to capture me. I often thrashed in bed, talking loud enough to wake Renee. This morning she was asleep on the living room sofa, so I decided to go for a walk on the beach. It was quiet and peaceful before the crush of tourists. The sky was dark, indigo on the edge of darkness, with a yellow-gold hint of sunrise spread across the horizon. The surf gently soothed my feet in foam, the receding tide coaxing me further into the water. I had played with my children on this beach, collecting shells, turning horseshoe crabs over to see if they were still alive. We'd spend hours searching for soft-shell crabs among the rock jetties, terrorizing petrels that scurried at the edge of the surf, defying the water as it reclaimed the shoreline. We were children together. Jo would watch us from her blanket and shake her head. What happened to our marriage?

AFTER LUNCH, RENEE AND HER MOTHER decided to go shopping, so I grabbed a book and went out to the sunroom to read. Not long after they left my phone rang.

"Pete, David Condon. How the hell are you, buddy?

"Okay, I guess," answering him reflexively.

I hadn't sorted out what Ronald had said the day before, and I was afraid that David was his tag-teammate, ready to hit me with an uppercut to the jaw.

"It's good to hear your voice. You don't sound any different."

"Well I'm not, David."

"What have you been doing with yourself?"

He didn't sound any different. He was crazy, totally nuts, the prankster of our class. He grew up in Brooklyn and fought his way out of the neighborhood. He was playing college football on a scholarship at Utah State when he bailed out looking for a taste of real life. I guess he thought he had found it in Special Forces, like the rest of us searching for a tribe. I told him the same story I had told Ronald.

When David got out of the service, he bought a motorcycle and headed across the country. I never realized it, but he had been a concert pianist. A few years after he got out of the service, he buried himself in his music, studying with an old teacher of his, and practiced hours and hours every day for months. He spent years traveling up and down the West Coast, getting odd jobs, playing gigs, partying, and moving on. He told me he had a lot of trouble with relationships and trust. The VA shrinks helped him out and he was doing okay for a while, but then his oldest son was shot and killed, an innocent bystander in a holdup in Brooklyn. He freaked out, started using heroin to numb the pain, and finally had a nervous breakdown about 12 years ago.

"Are you … are you okay now?"

"Yeah, now I have a wife and little girl I adore. I live up in the Oregon high country. It's beautiful here, man. You've got to come up; it's so peaceful."

This wasn't the crazy David I knew. I was thinking about our time in Training Group, becoming medics, and how our shared experiences brought us together in a brotherhood that transcended traditional boundaries. Even though I wasn't particularly close to either he or Ronald, I still felt that closeness, the unspoken bond, a willingness to put one's life on the line for one another.

There was a pause in our conversation and I thought about what Ronald had said the day before.

"You know, Ronald called me yesterday. I really didn't want to talk to him, but you know how he is. Before I knew it, the shit was flying. Is he really as fucked up as he says?"

"Yeah, man. I ran with him on and off for years, he's just hard to take in large doses. He exaggerates and he's a narcissist, but if it wasn't for him I wouldn't have filed a claim for PTSD."

I felt dizzy. The furniture in the room started to move and the colors of everything faded. I collapsed into an easy chair in my mother-in-law's living room, unable to move. Visions of Special Forces training and Nam and firefights raced through my mind like a runaway movie, no sound, just images, black and white, moving so fast that I couldn't focus on any of them. I couldn't concentrate and I had no control over them. I don't know how long this went on but I was startled when the kitchen door slammed as Renee and her mother came in from shopping. I looked around the living room. The movie had stopped. My clothing was soaked with perspiration and I shivered. I had a flashback for I don't know how long, at least an hour, because Renee had been gone for almost three hours. Before I could compose myself, Renee walked in and was stunned to see me slouched in the chair. The cell phone was lying on the floor.

"What's the matter? Are you okay … you're drenched; do you feel sick?" She came over to the chair and put her hand on my cheek, and looked into my eyes.

"I must have dozed off. David Condon, one of my medic classmates, called and we had a long conversation, but I don't remember what happened next. I must have fallen asleep."

"Honey, I'm worried about you. You haven't been yourself since that Ronald guy called. Are these conversations bringing back bad memories?"

"I … I don't know. I guess they are. I'm not encouraging them, but these memories are coming from somewhere. They haven't bothered me before."

The drive home to Syracuse was unsettling. It was a cool, clammy day, the sky overcast with thick gray clouds. It drizzled as we pulled onto Interstate 90 heading west. I was on autopilot, peeling away the chapters of my first marriage, still raw with emotion seven years after the divorce.

"You look like you're in a fog. Are you alright? What are you thinking about?" Renee asked.

Cars passed me on the highway as if I was standing still. I thought for a minute, not sure how to respond.

"Everything and nothing, Ronald and David, my divorce, my time in the service, my financial problems … I feel like my mind is trying to let me in on a secret."

Renee leaned over toward me, reached for my shoulder and caressed it. I could feel her warmth as she smiled at me. “Give it time, honey. Your mind will reveal those secrets when you’re ready.”

By the time we got home, I was exhausted. Night had fallen. I stumbled around the house parrying with memory fragments until I collapsed into bed.

David C

Back from the Cape, I felt like I'd had the sense slapped out of me; first Ronald, and then David. They're both collecting disability checks with comp ratings of 100 percent. These guys are screwed up big-time. What the hell happened to them in Nam? I was curious, because my memory was a blur. I decided to call David. We got into a conversation about some of the other guys from Training Group.

"Hey, do you remember Matt Wilson?"

"Yeah," I said. "What's he up to?"

Matt was an interesting guy. He had some college but was a bit immature like me. His father was some big shot, circuit court judge in Oregon who didn't like where Matt's life was headed. In protest, Matt joined Special Forces. I guess he showed his father!

"Yeah, I palled around with him for a few years after we got out, but he got really mean. He packed a pistol and more than once threatened his wife. He had a homestead up in the mountains in Oregon, and over time he became more withdrawn. The last time I saw him three years ago, his wife had called me in a panic asking for help. I told her to gather what she needed and I would be up to get her. I showed up only to face him down at the end of a shotgun barrel. She got out while I talked him down off the ledge, but he scared the shit out of me, man. He didn't realize that I'd helped his wife escape. He'd have killed me for sure if he knew. That's the last time I saw him. For all I know, he could be dead by now."

"What happened to him?"

"Matt never saw any serious action in Nam, but how many dead bodies do you need to see before it affects you. All I can tell you is that he's messed up."

"Hey, remember Billy Kopps?"

Do I remember Billy Kopps? He was the baddest guy in our class, six-foot-four and about 220. He had a look that could scare the bejesus out of you, and the coldest-looking eyes I've ever seen. He was a softie, but you couldn't cross him, because he had a mean streak as deep as a canyon, courtesy of his father, who beat the shit out of him and his brother regularly when they were growing up. He was the guy you'd go to if you needed an enforcer.

"Yeah, what's he doing?"

"He's dead. I think he committed suicide. They found his pickup truck at the bottom of a ravine up here in the high country; missed a turn and went right off the road into the treetops 300 feet below."

"What-the-fuck. What happened to him?"

His wife had left him and took his son. He begged her to stay, but I guess she'd had enough of his mood swings and temper. He was despondent. His family was everything to him. It was his only connection to sanity.

"Was he abusing her?"

"No, I don't think so. He adored her, but he'd get that look, that animal look, and it must have scared the shit out of her. He was a bad motherfucker when he was like that. We used to do gigs together; he played the fiddle and guitar. More than once, I saw him go off on someone. God help them. Billy saw a lot of action in the Delta. He wasn't the same afterward. Fact is none of us are."

"Did you know that Tommy Hawkins is MIA?"

"No. What happened?"

"The North Vietnamese overran his A-Camp and he and two others were taken hostage. It turned out that they were left behind in a mass evacuation of the camp. The C-Team Ops officer called in a napalm strike. Two days later, a search team found the crispy remains of an estimated company-sized enemy force, but they never confirmed the remains of the two Americans."

The news about Tommy made my gut wrench. He and I were close, sharing an off-post apartment at Fort Sam Houston while going through the second phase of our medical training. He was married with a kid, and at 27, older than most of us and more mature. We all looked up to him. Why would the C-Team have called in napalm before knowing the whereabouts of all Americans? I was incensed.

"Doesn't that figure, David: a trigger-happy desk jockey wanted to make a name for himself."

"Not unusual. I'll tell you sometime about some of the assholes I served with. They're lucky to be alive."

After I got off the phone, I thought about Perez and what had happened in that last firefight. I was angry, but I didn't know if I was angry at Perez, or myself.

It was about this time that the flashbacks really kicked in. There was no rhyme or reason to when I'd get a flashback. Casual things that happen during the course of the day would trigger them. I could be in a meeting with a client and an object on a shelf or a word spoken and I'd dissociate. The guy would be talking about his succession plan, and I'd be walking from my dispensary at Long Hai over to the Team House. I was hypervigilant. The banging lid on a dumpster would send me flying for cover. The smell of burning brush would bring me back to cooking fires in Nam. An Asian face in a crowd would startle me. I was angry all the time. Waiting at an intersection for a stoplight to turn, I'd grip the steering wheel seething in anger thinking about what I'd do if the guy behind me honked once the light changed. One day it happened. I jumped out of the car ready to pull the driver out of his seat, only to find an old woman cringing behind the wheel.

I was now having nightmares regularly. The one with the NVA chasing me was a regular, but not the worst. They were the ones where I had been captured and asked to answer questions that were forbidden by the Geneva Convention. You could tell them your name, rank, and service number, period. Giving any more information was strictly forbidden. Violate it and face retribution, that is, if you were fortunate enough to escape your captors. I wasn't the only soldier who obsessed about what questions to answer if he were captured. In my dream, the NVA had me strapped to a rickety bamboo table, naked. He'd ask me the name of my commanding officer while drawing his razor-sharp knife blade along the base of my scrotum. I'd wake up screaming just as he drew blood. Another was a scene where I had been captured, folded into a bamboo cage a cubic meter in size, and paraded through villages that had been ransacked by regular army soldiers. The villagers spat on me and children poked me with sticks.

Scenes from firefights and the god-awful smell of burning flesh were a frightful reminder that I would never have any peace. I was a hostage to my memories.

Memory

I'd always buried myself in work, and when I wasn't working, it was projects, the busy kind that shutter your mind and leave your body limp. I never could relax, not since Vietnam. I felt like I needed to have something to do every minute of every day. I was good at it. I had no control over my financial life, but I sure worked hard to control all other aspects of it. I went to the gym every morning and was in my office by 7:30 a.m. I worked long hours, but I couldn't work for others. It was a trust thing, like trusting your buddy to cover you while you're saving another soldier's life.

I was the patron saint of lost causes. My clients were small businesses in trouble that needed saving. My hobbies were projects that needed fixing, like old furniture, cars, and antique boats. The only difference between my life as a medic and my life as a civilian was the absence of blood. I never allowed myself to feel. After all, I was a Green Beret; we didn't feel, we acted, we did. But feelings nonetheless presented themselves. I lamented becoming a businessman, and not a doctor.

Whenever things slowed down in my life my mind would introduce me to my feelings, my emotions. I began to see that there was a person inside me who had been hiding for decades; an emotional, empathetic human being who had hidden behind an impenetrable veneer, protected from memories of war. The weeks after the Cape vacation were filled with these thoughts. Several more conversations with Ronald and David over the course of the summer before the September reunion made me think of the parallels between their lives and my own. The managers who betrayed my trust; the woman who betrayed my trust and divorced me; the people whom I thought were friends, but who just couldn't measure up. I felt lonely, abandoned, and confused.

When I got out of the service, I put all my army memorabilia in a box and stored it away, out of sight. I wanted no part of that memory to cloud my future. I would see the box every time we moved and try to decide whether to leave it behind, but the box followed me everywhere. I exchanged e-mails with other classmates as the time for the reunion approached and thought more and more about my memory box in the barn. It had been 15 years since I had last looked at my slides and pictures. I climbed the steps to the second floor of the barn where the box was stored. It was tucked in the corner under several other boxes, out of sight. I pulled it out, sat down on a stool and carefully unfolded the lid to expose the contents. There was the full-size map of Vietnam that my mother had given me when I was home on leave from the hospital, my medic handbook, and lots of small boxes with color slides and photos. As I flipped through them I was horrified at what I saw. There was a photo of my teammates and me huddled over the remains of a Viet Cong soldier we had killed on an ambush that night. He was a teenager, probably not more than 16 years old. There wasn't much left of his head and face, torn away by multiple gunshot wounds, the scene framed by the smiling faces of my teammates. There was a photo of me laughing, snuggled in a body bag with the corpse of another dead VC.

I felt a tremor in my hands and perspiration dripped off my forehead and onto the pictures. I began to heave uncontrollably and tossed the pictures on the floor, hoping to rid myself of the feeling of disgust that had overcome me. I was nauseous, even though I had seen these photos many times before.

After a few minutes, I pulled out my old berets, dog tags and a box of insignia, Class A brass, and other uniform stuff. Then I saw the gold-and-ivory Buddha amulet I was wearing around my neck the day I got hit. Next to it was the Khmer prayer cloth that was folded in my left breast pocket over my heart. I opened it up to look at the icons and designs, and wondered whether this piece of cloth was what saved my life? I opened a large envelope in the box and inside was my bloody blue, white, and red Mike Force scarf. I reached in and pulled out the scarf, still tied in a knot where it had hung around my neck and over my chest. I trembled as I held it up, then put it over my head and draped it over my shoulders. The colors were barely recognizable, the scarf stiff, saturated with my dried blood.

There were copies of citations awarding me the Bronze Star with 'V' device for valor and Purple Heart. There were citations from Special Forces Training Group, hailing and congratulating me for successful completion of training. And there was a framed copy of the Special Forces Aidman's Pledge that we took at the completion of our training, like the Hippocratic Oath taken by doctors.

I read it slowly aloud so I could hear the words:

> As a Special Forces Aidman of the United States Army, I pledge my honor and my conscience to the service of my country and the art of medicine. I recognize the

> responsibility, which may be placed upon me for the health, and even lives, of others. I confess the limitation of my skill and knowledge in caring for the sick and injured. I promise to follow the maxim "Primum non nocere" ("First, thou shalt do no harm"), and to seek the assistance of more competent medical authority whenever it is available. Those confidences, which come to me in my attendance on the sick, I will treat as secret. I recognize my responsibility to impart to others who seek the service of medicine such knowledge of its art and practice as I possess, and I resolve to continue to improve my capability to this purpose. As an American soldier, I have determined ultimately to place above all considerations of self the mission of my team and the cause of my nation.

I was struck by the utter incongruity of the statement. Had I been there to heal or to kill? The moral dilemma simmering for years beneath my consciousness suddenly erupted in the reality that as medics, we weren't expected to do the moral thing, to save human life. The mission always came first, and if that meant taking a human life, then so be it. I then realized the absurdity of my Vietnam experience.

I ripped the scarf off my neck, tossed it back in the box, and wept.

"Pete, are you up there … Pete?"

I opened my eyes to shadows of darkness. It was dusk, and the light shining through the window was the pink, gray and lavender of a fading sun. Groggy, I looked around and realized that I was in the barn.

"Pete, are you there?"

"Yes … yes, I'm up here."

"What are you doing there? Do you know what time it is?"

"No, I … I mean nothing."

I raised myself up on my elbow as Renee was climbing up the ladder. As her head came into view, she could see that I was reclining on the floor.

"Are you okay? What's going on?"

"Oh, nothing; I was just going through some of my stuff and got tired. I guess I must have fallen asleep."

She looked at me, my eyes still heavy with sleep, and probably puffy.

"What's going on, McShane? You look like you've been run over by a bus!"

I hesitated to answer, knowing what was going to come next. She stepped off the ladder, walked over, and sat down next to me.

"I was going through my Vietnam box."

"You never talk about Vietnam, or what's in the box. Are you okay, honey?"

"There's nothing to talk about. Besides, how could I talk to you about something that you couldn't possibly relate to? I mean you've never been in a war."

"You're right, I've never been to war, but I love you and it might help for you to talk about it with me. You trust me, don't you?"

This is it. What will she do when she knows what I know? She might leave me. And if I don't confide in her she'll know that I don't trust her … I've got to tell her. She has tremendous fortitude, having survived physical and emotional abuse by her first husband. I love and admire her. I glanced up at her pensively.

"I trust you."

She leaned over and hugged me. I felt the warmth of her body against mine, a calmness and serenity that I coveted. I hesitated for a moment and then pulled the box between us, turned on a table lamp, and opened the lid. The beam of light flowed into the box and illuminated its contents. As I showed her my effects, the memories came to life. I couldn't stop; there was no turning back.

I showed her the prayer cloth and the Buddha, and how Noh had given it to me as thanks for saving that child who had run into the minefield.

"Oh my God, Pete. You risked your life to save that boy?"

"Yeah. My team sergeant wasn't any too happy, either."

"Why?"

"He didn't want me risking my life for our strikers or their families."

She ran her fingers over the images on the cloth and fingered the gold-and-ivory Buddha.

"This is beautiful."

"The Khmer Kampuchea Krom are a superstitious, but spiritual people. The monks blessed the prayer cloth and the Buddha amulet, and our strikers carried them. When we got into a firefight, they would put the amulet in their mouth, believing that the Buddha would protect them."

I reached into the box to return the envelope with the Buddha amulet and prayer cloth, and as I did, Renee caught a glimpse of the bloody scarf.

"What's that, honey?"

"It's what I was wearing around my neck when I got hit."

She reached in to touch it, then she picked it up, cupping it in her hands gently, as if cradling an infant, and looked up at me with tearful eyes.

"Oh, Pete …"

Tears were streaming down Renee's cheek. She reached over, wrapped her arms around me, and rested her head on my shoulder. I could feel her tremble.

"What was it like during firefights? Were you scared?"

"I've never been so frightened in my life. But you know what; I've never been so exhilarated. It's weird. I hated every minute of it, but I found myself wanting to go back and do it again."

"What do you mean?"

"Combat is the ultimate adrenaline rush. It's bone-chilling terror, pure and simple. Your opponent wants to kill you, and the feeling is mutual. It's difficult to convey the fear I felt to anyone who hasn't experienced it firsthand. It defies explanation. Training taught us to focus on our objective. The initial fear was greatest at the beginning of the action but, after that, I was able to block out the fear and do my job. After you've been in several firefights, you could actually feel the rush of adrenaline coursing through your veins as the fear began to permeate every inch of your being. Fear can turn you into a catatonic bundle of nerves, or a puddle of fecal matter. It's all about mind control.

"I often wondered why so many SF guys did two and three tours in Nam. Every time you escaped injury, you couldn't wait for the next operation. It was addictive. You felt immortal, like you were cheating the gods. The military has it all figured out. Go after the young Turks, brimming with testosterone and looking to test their mettle. War suits the bill just fine. Show them a picture of a paratrooper jumping out of a plane, or a soldier rappelling from a helicopter, and you've got them hooked. That's how they get guys to sign up for hazardous duty. Then there's the aftermath of the firefight, the death and dying part. They wouldn't get any recruits if they showed them pictures of how they'd look in a fucking body bag."

"Why did you sign up for Special Forces anyway?"

I told her about Maddy Madison, a neighbor back home, and the stories about his A-Camp and what Special Forces medics did in the field.

"I wanted to be a doctor and I thought the experience would help me later on when I applied for med school.

I DUG DEEPER INTO THE BOX and pulled out the framed Aidman's Pledge.

"What really kills me is this oath that we took as medics."

I passed the 8×10 frame to Renee.

"They spent a full year training us to play doctor in the field, to tend to our mercenaries and their families. But they were expendable. Our first duty was to support the mission, which was to kill the enemy, and the second was to keep our teammates alive. Not only was this pledge a farce, our military mission in Vietnam was a mistake. The irony is that we were the enemy. The Vietnamese didn't want us there. The Diem government was a sham, propped up by the US. After the Viet Minh crushed the French at Dien Bien Phou, the Paris Peace Accords called for the Vietnamese people to vote on the repatriation of the north and the south. That vote never happened, because the US was obsessed with stopping the spread of communism in Indochina. We didn't give a shit about what the Vietnamese people wanted. We should never have gone to war."

Almost a minute passed while she read the pledge.

"The Cambodes were expendable?"

"I didn't carry life-saving supplies like IVs for them, and we only medevaced Americans."

"My God. How could you do that?"

"Orders. I had no choice … believe me, I tried."

She handed the pledge back while shaking her head.

"Weren't they anticommunist?"

"Yes, but not because they were concerned about the spread of communism; they wanted their homeland back."

"What?"

"In 1970, our A-Camps and Mike Force operations were turned over to the South Vietnamese, part of Nixon's political fix—Vietnamization. He had Kent State to deal with, and was desperately trying to reduce our presence in Nam. We were forbidden to provide military support to the Khmer Krom, and we sent them back to Cambodia alone to support Lon Nol's coup against Sihanouk. He was unable to pull the disparate fighting elements together in a unified effort against the North Vietnamese and bungled operation after operation at a tremendous loss of lives. It all ended with the communist Khmer Rouge and the North Vietnamese crushing Krom resistance, which ultimately led to the fall of South Vietnam in 1975. We turned our backs on them. Our Cambodes were slaughtered. I feel responsible."

"How have you dealt with all this, I mean, the memories?"

"The only thing I could do—push them away."

Renee leaned over, kissed me on the cheek and whispered, "I'm so sorry."

We sat in silence while she stroked my arm. I'd never talked to anyone about this before, about how I felt. Curiously, I was at peace, the way I felt after confessing my sins to a priest.

VA Shrink

The innocuous label in the lobby said "Behavioral Health". Standing in an elevator full of people, a month before the reunion, I didn't want to be seen pushing that button, but there I was at 60 years old, seeing a shrink for the first time in my life.

I had heard vets talk about the eighth floor of the VA Medical Center. It was for the nut cases who made civilians nervous. I thought they might have been joking until I stepped off the elevator. There weren't any examining rooms or weight scales in the hallway, and no hospital smell. It looked like a floor in an office building, far removed from the typical clinics and the daily bustle of the hospital, except for the VA cop stationed near the front desk. After checking in, I sat in a waiting room with vets who didn't feel dangerous, but rather pensive and subdued. One of them kept rubbing his hands together like he was cold. Another, with long greasy hair and dressed in old fatigues, just stared at the floor. There was no eye contact and no conversation.

I kept asking myself why I was here. Once labeled with PTSD, I might as well say I was mentally ill. But after listening to my medic buddies, I knew something was wrong with me, that there must be a reason for all the things that had happened in my life since returning from Vietnam. I suspected I had some problems, but had never considered that I could be mentally ill. Green Berets don't go mental, I told myself. But after the conversations with David and Ronald, I began to think otherwise. I realized that their symptoms weren't just the ravings of two crazy GIs. VA counselors had told them that Green Beret medics had a high incidence of PTSD, and there is nothing shameful in admitting it. Unlike other medics in the service, we carried weapons and were expected to use them. Anyway, I'd have to cop to the symptoms if I had any hope of getting more disability compensation. I had been at 40 percent since 1969, based on my wounds. Agent Orange-related diabetes pushed it to 50 percent in 2002.

Doctor Moffett, a retired Army psychiatrist, came out to the waiting room to meet me. About my age, he was also a professor at the medical college, which was common at the VA. His specialty was addiction, and I wondered how I had wound up in his office. It was large for the VA, and the memorabilia of his life filled it. His medical degree was displayed prominently on one wall next to a doctorate in chemistry, and a master's in something. Three or four Board Certifications, accolades, and photos absent any evidence of military service covered the rest of the wall, a mosaic of plate glass reflections. There was no couch or recliner in the room.

Standing in front of a bookcase displaying reference manuals, he was chatty and contemplative in a way I hadn't expected. There was regret as he talked about the routine of his military career counseling drunken soldiers. I couldn't tell if he was feeling sorry for himself, or regretful that he couldn't have done more for his patients. We had Catholicism in common, both of us having had a vocational calling to the priesthood earlier in life. He had abandoned the Church for Native American spirituality, while I had simply fallen away.

Since my primary care physician at the VA had referred me, the doctor asked me what was on my mind.

"I think I have PTSD."

He gave me a curious look. Then he started firing questions like, "Are you hypervigilant?" "Are you angry or depressed?" "Have you tried to kill yourself?" I felt like he was reading from a checklist of symptoms, marking the ones that applied to this veteran. I didn't know how to respond, and was getting agitated. I gestured with my arms outstretched, palms opened wide.

"Where do I start? I've talked to buddies who have PTSD, and their problems are familiar—they're my problems."

Sitting at a small round table in the middle of the room, Moffett was momentarily distracted by someone's knock at the door. I thought that it might be some predetermined signal, that if he didn't answer, the cop would burst in with weapon drawn. He yelled, "I'm with a client," and looked at me. "Sorry. Alright, can you be more specific?"

I felt the room closing in.

"Okay. I have no friends. My employment history is checkered. I don't trust anyone. I pushed my wife away; we hadn't had sex in at least 10 years, now we're divorced. I've suspected for some time that there's something wrong with me."

He smiled, as if relieved.

"You've just told me symptoms that could apply to every human being on earth." He chuckled.

What the fuck is so funny?

"Let's drill down on specifics. Do you have trouble sleeping?"

"I don't know. I … I guess I do. I used to grind my teeth. I think I still do. Sometimes I'll wake up at night drenched in perspiration. I have some bad dreams."

"Do you get upset easily?"

"Oh, yeah. I'm intolerant, especially of incompetent people."

"Tell me about your employment history."

I told him how I couldn't trust my bosses. They lied to me, but they expected me to trust them. They made me angry. I either bailed, was asked to leave, or was fired. Moffett looked at me like I was crazy.

"Sometimes we have to do things we don't like. That's why they call it work," he said, smiling. I felt like punching him.

"What's your definition of trust?"

I thought for a few seconds.

"I think of my buddies in Special Forces, men who watched my back, men who put their lives on the line for me. I did the same for them."

Moffett pursed his lips, his eyes shifting to the ceiling for a moment.

"And you apply that standard to choosing friends and people in the workplace?"

"Yes."

"Don't you think that you're being too critical? After all, we're all human. We're not infallible. Can't you give people a break?"

"No."

My answers befuddled him. I suppose it's difficult for anyone to understand the extraordinary degree of personal commitment my teammates had for one another. Anything less than that threatened our mission. It's no wonder that people back-on-the-block continually disappointed me. His brow furrowed as he took a deep breath.

"Can you tell me about your worst memory of Vietnam?"

His intrusive questioning annoyed me. He knew my branch of service and that I had served in combat, and was wounded. Why did he need to ask me for detail that was already in my medical record?

"You mean other than being shot in the chest and wondering whether I was going to live?"

"Okay, good," said Moffett.

"And then, hanging in a McGuire rig below a chopper and the winch malfunctions; watching muzzle flashes from the jungle below, the NVA guns trying to finish me off."

Moffett never twitched as he made notes on his legal pad.

"How did that experience make you feel?"

"I can't remember having any feelings."

Deeply embarrassed, I had never discussed what happened that day with loved ones, much less total strangers. The doctor leaned back in his chair and paused for a few seconds.

"Sounds like posttraumatic stress disorder—you present the symptoms."

Hearing him say the words was a bit of a shock, even though I knew they would come. It was the realization that I was certifiable. Summarizing my symptoms for Moffett had brought the memories of a lifetime into focus: I had lost my family. I cared for no one. I couldn't keep a job. I was bankrupt. I was a failure.

Moffett said that until 1980, posttraumatic stress disorder wasn't considered a medical condition. Up until then, if a veteran had the symptoms, he was given antidepressants and sleep meds, and told to get some rest. If he persisted, he was labeled a mental case.

"Problem is that we don't have any medications to treat the condition, specifically. We have to treat it symptomatically. I can prescribe Wellbutrin for anger management, Celexa for depression, and Ambien for sleep."

He went on about how Celexa, Welbutrin, and other SSRIs have been shown effective in helping slow patients' reaction to stimuli. As he was explaining the chemical reactions and their effects on the nervous system, I remember David and Ronald having said that the VA simply threw drugs at the problem. Now I believed them. It sounded to me like things hadn't changed any since 1980.

"While these medications don't necessarily affect the libido, I can also prescribe Viagra. What do you think?"

I pushed my hands through my hair, clasping them at the base of my skull, and glanced at the ceiling. This is therapy? Take drugs?

"Doctor, I need to think about all of this. For 35 years, I've rejected the thought that there's something wrong with me. I just figured that my life was all about bad luck. When my buddies told me their problems, I thought they were weak. They're fucked up, not me. But now I know differently."

He got up from the table with a flourish, like the hard work was finished, and sat behind his desk.

"We can treat your symptoms, but that's the extent of it. PTSD doesn't go away. Over time, a successful treatment modality should provide you with the tools to manage the symptoms."

"That's it? You've told me about the drugs. What about counseling?"

"Our clinical psychologist, Doctor Walden, is starting a new vets group, all Vietnam-era. Would you like to call her?"

I shook my head. "I'm confused. This sounds like a self-treatment regime."

He leaned back in his chair.

"It's up to you to follow through. Group therapy is a good place to start. You and I can meet again in 90 days and see how you're doing. And we can talk about meds then, if you like. How's that?"

I wondered what kind of counseling do you get every 90 days?

"Doctor, frankly I was expecting more today."

"Well, your symptoms suggest that you're not a threat to yourself or others. Under those conditions, group therapy can be very effective. Why don't we try that before we move on to individual counseling?"

Before I left, he showed me how to do deep breathing exercises if I got anxious or angry, and he wrote me a script for fish oil capsules. I thought it was a joke—so much for psychiatric counseling. So much for the VA's behavioral health program. I'm on my own.

After the appointment, I remembered the drugs David told me he had taken, like Prozac, Zoloft, Celexa, Wellbutrin, Ambien, and others. Some of them weren't even on the VA formulary. He'd get them from a civilian doctor, or on the street. I kept thinking about the term Moffett used, "Manage the symptoms." For whose benefit? Keep the lid on crazy vets like me—dumb us down with drugs? No thank you.

Reunion

Reno lies in an arid valley nestled in the Sierra Nevada Mountains. It's perfectly flat for as far as you can see, the surrounding mountains hiding behind an ever-present bluish-yellow haze. You can see the city from afar growing up out of the desert like manmade cacti. It was five thirty in the evening, and the lights of the casinos ignited the sky with unnatural colors, giving the city an eerie, out-of-this-world look. Tired-looking hotels stood brick to brick with garish monstrosities, lurking in the glow of millions of electric lights in pastels and primaries. Floodlights perched high on cornices, as in a prison courtyard, followed the creatures on the street, coaxing, lulling, threatening to reach down and sweep them from the sidewalks into the casinos.

The Sand Pebble was off the strip, though it was probably on the strip 30 years ago when it was built. We parked the car in the lot down the street and dragged our bags into the vestibule. I felt like we had stepped into a subterranean world. The lobby was a cacophony of sights, sounds, and smells; full of slot machines and old women with cigarettes dangling from their lips, jerking off the machines in hopes of a reward. People in shorts, sport coats and suits, formal dresses and T-shirts mingled, fixated on cards and dice at gambling tables. The air was heavy with the smell of stale tobacco and body odor. Decades of smoke had tinged the walls and ceilings a pale yellow, giving the lobby a burnished, tired look. It was purgatory, the perfect venue for a reunion of soldiers.

Renee and I made our way to the room, a nonsmoking one, at least while we were there. It was now six thirty and I was getting nervous. There was an open house scheduled in a meeting room two floors up, and the moment of truth was near.

"When do you want to go to the open house?" I asked, hoping that she would suggest we have some dinner first.

"Why don't we go up now, visit for a while and then see what everyone is doing for dinner."

That's what I thought she'd say. Renee has a nice way of pulling my head out of the sand.

"Okay, let's go," I said.

Off we went, my palms sweating and my heart pounding. You'd have thought I was meeting the President of the United States the way I fretted about this encounter with my classmates. I didn't know what to expect—revelation or rebuke. We walked into the meeting room, and there were a handful of men and women, and I wondered whether we had come to the right place. Just then, someone shouted to me from the far corner of the room.

"Pete … Hey, Pete!"

An older, heavier Ronald Stoddard came up to me. We hesitated, shook hands and embraced, as easy as that.

"How was your flight in, buddy?"

"It was long but uneventful. Hey, I want you to meet my better half, Renee."

She presented herself to Ronald, extended her hand and he shook it gently.

"Pleasure to meet you, ma'am."

"Call me Renee."

"Is everyone in yet?" I said.

"No, there are a couple of the guys coming in later tonight, and one or two tomorrow morning before our meeting. The schedule is sort of loosey-goosey. This is an informal, low budget deal. I'm paying the freight for the meeting room and amenities. I'm hoping we can split the expenses once all the numbers are tallied up."

"No problem. Hey, is David here yet?"

"Yeah, he got in early this afternoon. He should be down soon."

I went over to the bar, cracked a bottle of beer, tilted my head back and let half of it run straight down my throat. I felt an immediate buzz at the base of my cranium, whether the effect of the cold beverage or the alcohol, I knew not, but it was welcome. Guys drifted in and I mingled nervously, sensing the same reluctance in others. I finished my beer and another, and felt more at ease. I recognized most of the guys, but the names were more of a challenge. That didn't matter. There was an ease in how we communicated that was comfortable, familiar, even after all these years. It wasn't just the talk, it was the body language, the inflections in our voices, the sincerity. There was a time when we would have trusted each other with our lives. It felt like the trust was still there.

"Pete?"

I looked around. David had entered the room and was walking toward me. His hair was gray and he had a goatee. I wasn't in his circle of friends in Training Group, but that had changed. Something seemed to bond us now that wasn't there before, a closeness.

The next morning came early. Renee and I had breakfast in the diner off the lobby of the hotel. She had plans to sightsee and would be gone all day. I didn't know how long our meeting would last, and told her to come up to the room later in the afternoon.

"How do you feel about this meeting?"

"Pretty good. There will be some guy from the Special Forces Association who was a VA Pension and Compensation claims service officer. After that, I'm not sure. I feel comfortable with the guys, but we also haven't gotten into any heavy discussions. I guess I'll just have to wait and see."

"Hope the meeting goes well. See you later. Love you."

The meeting room was much more crowded than the night before. More guys had arrived, and we did the obligatory introductions. Bob McCann came in just before the meeting started. We shook hands and chatted for a while, small talk about family, kids, and work. He had just come from San Antonio, where he had attended his daughter's graduation from law school. Bob had remarried ten years previously, and his daughter was from his first marriage. He had just retired from National Brewery, and was part-timing it with a local microbrewery.

Ronald opened the meeting with some general announcements and then introduced retired Master Sergeant Billy Dillworth, a long-time Green Beret. He lost a leg in the battle of Khe Sanh. After he retired, he went to work for the Veterans Administration, the guy who decided whether your disability claim was worthy. Several of us already had service-connected compensation, but most of the guys didn't, either from ignorance or stubbornness. Some of us still believed that Green Berets didn't need help from anyone.

"I want you guys to know that I hold you medics in the highest regard. There is no nobler endeavor than to serve your fellow teammates. The man who saved my life at Khe Sanh is sitting right over there."

He shifted his gaze to the corner of the room and asked Rob Knight to stand up. The room erupted in applause. Rob was from an earlier class in Training Group. I never knew him, but apparently he had made a career in Special Forces as a medic. After he retired, he went to work as a contractor with Halliburton running dispensaries in Iraq and Afghanistan.

"I want to thank Rob for saving my life, even though I had to tell him what to do! I think I was his first casualty."

Some of us laughed, but I sensed guys were holding back, not sure how to respond. I could feel pent-up emotional energy in the room, like not all of us were ready to let go.

"An incoming mortar round shattered my knee and lower leg, and it was hanging by sinew. Rob gingerly began telling me that I was going to be alright, and I yelled, 'cut the sweet talk, and clamp off the fucking bleeders!'"

We cracked up. I felt the room loosening up.

"Seriously, there is no more important job on an A-Team than Medical Aidman. You guys keep us healthy and alive. I hold my beret off to you."

After a round of questions, Ronald said he was available afterward to talk to any of the guys about his experience navigating the VA Compensation and Pension bureaucracy. We took a short break, arranged the chairs in a circle, and all 18 of us sat facing one another. Ronald suggested that we say whatever came to mind. There was an uncomfortable lull, a hesitation born of uneasiness. Larry Newton started out with an innocuous summary of his life since Training Group, with the names of his children, the schools they went to and the names of his grandchildren. It was comfortable, nonintrusive and easy to spit out. The next guy followed suit with the same storyline. Who wants to know this shit? I was concerned that we would accomplish nothing at this reunion.

David was the next guy in the circle. He began with the slow and measured report of a man who had told his story before.

"I was assigned to SOG out of Nha Trang. We ran covert ops into Laos to harass and interdict the NVA along the Ho Chi Minh Trail. It was brutal, man. There was a lot of incompetence, and I finally told the CO that I would not go out on any more missions. He agreed to my face, but you know what the deal is with medics. No one wants to go out on a mission without one of us. I told him that I had had enough and wanted to work in the dispensary. A week later, he asked me if I would go out on a recon mission, just over the border, to check out a suspected buildup of NVA at an old base camp that we had abandoned a month prior. He told me that it wasn't a hot assignment and pleaded with me to go, that it would be the last he would ask me to do. I reluctantly agreed.

"There were three of us, a second lieutenant and a staff sergeant who were both new to the Group. We inserted into an LZ in Laos, about 15 klicks over the border, and it turned out to be hot. As soon as the chopper touched down, we were hit with small arms fire. We ran like hell to cover about 20 meters off the LZ, and the NCO right next to me was shaking like a leaf. Turns out the guy was a desk jockey from the C-team out to earn his CIB. He had no combat experience, and neither did the lieutenant, who was fresh from OCS! I had two newbies on a hot mission and I was the seasoned soldier, the Spec Four medic. I was fucking pissed.

"Intel had been right about the enemy's position and strength, but operations had located the LZ right next to the perimeter of their base camp. I thought we were fucked. We were getting shot at from all directions. I called in gunships to strafe the area around the LZ in hopes that we could get that chopper back to extract us. The Cobras brought the wrath of God down on them, stunning them long enough for us to get the fuck outta there.

"When I got back to base, I burst into the CO's office, walked up to him, and toe to toe stuck my finger into his sternum and told him to never, ever send me out on a mission again. The next day, I was on a chopper to Khe Sanh. I got my wish for dispensary duty."

The room was dead still. David sat staring into the center of the room. He then looked up and proceeded.

"I didn't know what war was until Khe Sanh. It was three months of hell. I got in touch with my humanity fast. I was a bundle of nerves, a puddle of shit, and so were all the other Green Beanies up there. My life has been a disaster since getting out of the service. I have trouble with authority figures, don't trust anyone, and can't have loving relationships. I was hooked on heroin and had a nervous breakdown. I've got PTSD and am 100-percent disabled. The VA says that I can have a normal life. They give me pills but the nightmares don't go away."

An uneasy silence came over the room, like all the air had been sucked out. Guys nervously shifted in their seats, looked at the floor or around the room. I didn't know whether it was the shock of David's words or others' words trying to escape.

Ronald carried on from there.

"I was at Khe Sanh during the siege when David was there. That was when it all began for me. When I got out of the service, I couldn't handle civilian life. There was no one to talk to about what I saw, what I did; no one could understand. I've experienced the same thing. Dead-end jobs, a broken marriage, nervous breakdown, I've been there. Therapy has helped me, but I'm not the same guy you all knew in Training Group."

Tim Hutchens spoke next. He was assigned to an A-Camp in the Delta. After he ETS'd, he went back to college and law school and played attorney for about 20 years. Over time he realized the absurdity of our mission in Vietnam, and he became an antiwar activist, doing sit-ins at military bases, marching and otherwise making his feelings known publicly. He spoke openly now.

"It hit me after I began looking carefully at some of the operations we conducted. We used to set up ambushes at night on trails and roads near our camp, because no one but Charlie traveled at night. How do you think I felt when a woman and her son came to my sick call the morning after one ambush only to find out that

I had killed her husband the night before? I have tried to push the memory of that day into the far reaches of my mind, but it keeps coming back."

Some of the guys had relatively quiet assignments, and I could see they were incredulous. Then it was my turn. I felt a surge of energy, the same feeling a boxer must have when the bell is rung for the next round. I was fearful that some of the guys might not react well, but I had to let my story out. I explained what the Mike Force did and how I was told that I'd be setting up a regional hospital, but that instead, I spent all of my time in the field bailing out troubled A-Camps and doing H&I missions into Cambodia.

"I'm lucky to be alive today. I took an AK round in the chest during my last firefight. The round missed my heart by a few millimeters."

I paused a few moments while the shock of the words settled in the room.

Facial expressions changed as I told them what happened with Perez and how the doubts about my performance under fire festered like a weeping pustule. I told them about what our strikers did to prisoners, and how the team sergeant had chewed me out for saving that kid in the minefield.

"That Hippocratic oath we took was a fucking ruse. We were tools of war, tools of the government. Geneva Convention? Forget about it. I feel like a moral reprobate."

A few of the guys shifted in their seats, perhaps because I had rung a familiar chord. I went on to tell them how my dream of becoming a doctor ended on the SU campus, and chasing money became my life, how I pushed away my wife and had been bankrupt.

"It wasn't until I talked to Ronald and David that I realized what a disaster my life has been. I went to see a VA shrink last month and was diagnosed with PTSD. I feel angry and betrayed."

The room was dead silent. Tears streamed down my cheeks. I felt relieved, almost elated that I had spoken my mind, but wondered what impact my words had had on my classmates. I glanced around the room and surveyed faces, looking for signs of disbelief or disapproval, but saw none. Even though some had not come to grips with what they had done in Vietnam, no one denigrated those of us who had. Others wiped tears from their eyes.

"Hey, man, you didn't do anything wrong," yelled Roger Wilson, who had been stationed at the C-Team dispensary in Nha Trang.

"There was a lot of shit going on that we had no control over. You did what you felt was right, and I'm glad you made it home."

Others chimed in with their own endorsements, and local conversations ensued. Danny Phfluger, who had been stationed in the Delta came over and sat down next to me.

"Hey, I have a whole different way of thinking about you. I know we weren't that close in Group, but I'd like to get to know you better."

"Sure, Danny."

"As you, David, and Ronald talked about your lives since Nam, it never occurred to me that my life had been impacted by what I did and saw. Shit, man, I've been divorced. I have trouble with relationships; I'm a son-of-a-bitch sometimes to my live-in girlfriend. I'm surprised she's stuck with me. I don't trust others. Now I wonder whether I should see a shrink."

By now, everyone was milling around talking in small groups. I could see that the first round of show-and-tell had hit the mark.

After a 10-minute break, we sat back down, and continued around the room. Charlie Dunn had somehow missed the class draft for Vietnam, and spent the rest of his time in the 3rd Group dispensary at Bragg.

"I am ashamed that I never went to Nam. I've spent all these years feeling guilty. I want to apologize to you, to all of you, for not sharing your burden, and I'm so glad that you guys made it back." He broke down.

Almost in unison, the rest of us came to his defense.

"Charlie, we all share feelings of guilt. I feel guilty for not doing more to help our mercenary families. I feel guilty for leaving my team when they needed me most. I feel guilty for not giving IVs to our mercenaries. We were all thrust into situations in which we had no control," I said.

"It wasn't your decision to stay at Bragg," Ronald said. "The fact that we're all feeling guilty about something speaks to who we are as individuals. The government trained us as killers, but how do you take a group of empathetic, sensitive young men, train them to save lives, and then ask them to kill another human being?"

We spent ten hours in that meeting room, telling our stories, consoling one another, and bonding in a way that I never anticipated. At the end of the day, I realized how very glad I was to have gone to the reunion. For the first time since leaving Nam, I felt at peace with myself. There was no question about trust. These men were my brothers. This was my tribe.

I laid in bed that evening, thinking about the day's journey. It had been exhausting.

"I haven't had a chance to talk with you since the meeting. How did it go?" Renee asked softly.

I had a dull pain in the pit of my stomach all day long, and it hadn't gone away. It kept gnawing at me.

"It was the most intense emotional experience of my life. I'm numb. All these years since Training Group and Nam and I've been reunited with the people I trusted most in my life. Contrast that with the number of true friends I have made since getting out of the service; you know the number—zero. My mind is going around and around searching for answers. I feel apprehension, like I want to make up for lost time. I don't want to leave these guys. They're my brothers. If there is anyone on this earth who knows where

I've been, it's them. I feel a sense of comfort and relief. I just can't explain it, honey. I feel at peace and I don't want to lose it. I had no idea what to expect with the reunion meeting, and now I'm totally overwhelmed, exhausted, elated. My emotions are right on the surface of my skin."

"I'm so glad that you decided to go, and I'm glad that you wanted me to join you."

She hugged me tightly.

PART IV

THERAPY AND HEALING

Despair

Posttraumatic stress? I couldn't appreciate what that meant until I returned from the reunion. It was like going over a waterfall and plunging into a bottomless pool of depression. I was devastated. I didn't want to leave my buddies. I felt a comfort, a peace I had not experienced in years. Nightmares and flashbacks intensified.

After the reunion, I holed up in my home office writing everything I could remember about my life in the service, and what happened afterward. Those few days were a blur. I felt a gnawing pain in my gut, the sort of thing I thought was reserved for loved ones who've been separated. I had been separated … from the few men in my life I truly trusted. I was in trouble. After a week I was out of words. I was having trouble concentrating at work. I didn't want to go out in public. I was becoming a recluse. I had to talk to David. I punched in his number on my cell, hoping he'd picked up.

"Hey, buddy, how are you doing?" he said.

"Not good. I've been in a fog since the reunion. I can't think straight, can't work."

"Your memories starting to come out?"

"Yeah, I feel like I'm watching an old newsreel. I'll remember one thing and another memory will come crashing in. Where are they coming from?"

"Your subconscious, man. It's a wondrous thing; it protects us from ourselves, then when we least expect it … POW!"

"I'm having nightmares almost every night. I don't remember having any until I started digging for answers after our first conversation in May."

"There's that subconscious again. Have you asked your shrink for sleeping pills? Ambien is on the VA formulary. That's what I used to take."

"No, I haven't seen him since my first visit in August. That's when he told me I had PTSD. I was sleeping okay then."

"Call him and tell him what's going on. He'll prescribe it. How's everything else, I mean, how do you feel?"

I'd had lunch with Keith the day before and he told me that Jo had just been diagnosed with stage IV uterine cancer, she only had a few months to live. I felt guilty about shutting her out emotionally. I told David I was depressed.

"Hey, man, it takes two to dance. I know how you feel, but you couldn't help how you behaved. Remember your subconscious? Call it your orchestra conductor; it's behind your actions and behaviors. Don't blame yourself."

"Easy for you to say."

"It is, man. I've done it to every important woman in my life, too. It's painful, but don't blame yourself."

"I feel angry, so angry. We were fed the government party line, you know, the vile North Vietnamese and the Domino Theory bullshit. The Vietnamese people didn't need us meddling in their lives. How fucking gullible were we?"

"I don't know about you, but I didn't join Special Forces to fight the commies. It was all in the timing, just like everything else in life; there just happened to be a war for us to get drawn into. My old man used to say 'Be a man'. He and his brothers fought in WWII. They strutted around like peacocks with their chests puffed out. Yeah, the government lied to us, but what's new. Governments have been manipulating their subjects since the beginning of time."

I told him about my father, who failed the military physical, and his little brother the war hero. I needed to prove something to my father, show him what a real man was made of.

"Hey, have you filed a claim for PTSD yet?"

"I'm working on it. Filing the claim for Agent Orange diabetes was easy compared to this. What a pain-in-the-ass. They want proof that I was in a combat zone: names, dates, and places. Come on, I've been collecting disability comp for 36 years for my wounds. What more proof do they need that I saw combat?"

"That's how the VA manages the process. They make it difficult to get compensation, to flush out the posers. I'm sure you've run into them; there are guys out there who are great actors. Some of them haven't had a fucking shot fired at them. That's who you're competing with."

"That sucks. What about the poor guys who have been damaged but don't have the patience to go through the mill?"

"It's one less claim to process and one less check to send out. The VA's got a budget. Put everything you can remember down on paper. Give them as much detail as you can remember: names of operations, firefights, and any other events that caused trauma. Be as specific as you can, and include verification from others you served with about your experiences."

"Man, talk about overkill. I'll put a narrative together, but a lot of it I can't remember. I mean, how much detail do they need?"

"Go for overkill; make it easy for them to give you the rating. You deserve 100 percent. I went through three claims before I got 100 percent. My first was 30 percent. I filed the second claim with more specific detail, and I was going to group therapy sessions by then. But I was heavy into drugs, man. I filed and got 70 percent.

In order to get to 100 percent, I got letters from my CO verifying the firefights and the nastiness, and I wrote a 17-page narrative about how PTSD had fucked up my life. Before I filed, I had a nervous breakdown. That was after my son got killed—bingo. One hundred percent."

"How long did the process take, David?"

"If you include my early efforts for treatment, 20 years."

"What? Are you fucking kidding me?"

"No, man. I first started going to the VA just after I got out in '69. Back then, there was no such thing as PTSD. They called it shell-shock, or combat fatigue, but these weren't acknowledged as medical conditions. So, the docs would give us antidepressants and sleeping meds to shut us up. There was no therapy. It wasn't until 1980 that the psychiatric community recognized PTSD as a bona fide medical condition. My final claim was adjudicated in '96."

"Yeah, like exposure to Agent Orange. How many of us fucking grunts had to die with lymphoma or diabetes without treatment or compensation before the VA acknowledged all the diseases it had caused?"

"That's just the way it is, man; government in action. One thing to remember: don't yell or disrespect your counselors; they're there to help you. They have to deal with the bureaucracy as well. You'll get a lot farther by keeping calm and asking them for help. Guys who yell and scream get nowhere. Hey, you need to talk with Ronald about claim filing. He is the expert; he helped me."

"Okay. Later, man."

I got off the phone with David somewhat relieved, but I could feel the knot in my stomach getting tighter as I thought about what I was going to have to do to get the treatment I needed and fair compensation. How was I going to earn a living now that I was an emotional basket case? I couldn't face myself in the mirror;

how could I face my clients? But I wasn't convinced that I was bad enough to get a 100-percent rating.

I called Ronald the next day and he told me the same thing David had. He suggested having one of the service organizations like the Disabled American Veterans or the Military Order of the Purple Heart help me. A week later, I met with a service officer from MOPH and we put the PTSD claim together. I was expecting a four-to-six month wait. To my surprise, two weeks later, in mid-October, I got my answer: the VA form letter said based on the available evidence, my disability rating was set at 30 percent. I was livid. I immediately made an appointment at the MOPH office.

As I counted the days to the meeting, I couldn't understand the VA's logic; I thought I had provided plenty of evidence to support a higher claim. When I met with the service officer, he could see that I was agitated. He was new in the job, and I was probably the first guy to yell at him. He summoned the office manager, a woman in her late 60s, a retired VA nurse. She looked like a drill instructor, short and barrel-chested with neatly trimmed hair and a military demeanor. Evelyn Blodgett was her name. She was the resident expert in claims filing and proceeded to tell me that I should be happy with the rating I received. I exploded.

"How can you say that I've been treated fairly? Have you read the material that I submitted in support of my claim?"

"No, I haven't. I don't need to. I understand how the system works. First of all, how long has it been since you were diagnosed with PTSD?"

"It's been 60 days."

"Who is seeing you in Psychiatric Services?"

"Doctor Moffett, the shrink," I said.

"How many appointments have you had?"

"One."

"Have you had any other services, like group counseling, or one-on-one appointments with one of the psychologists or clinical social workers?"

"No."

"Then that's the reason for the 30-percent rating. You're lucky you got that and in record time, I might add."

I was taken aback with the forcefulness of her attack. She disarmed me. I had no defense.

"My symptoms have gotten much worse. I went to a reunion in September, and now I'm falling apart emotionally."

"Mr. McShane, let me tell you how the system works. First off, it's up to your doctor to establish the severity of your PTSD symptoms. Mild to moderate symptoms can be rated from zero to 30 percent; moderate: 30 to 70 percent and severe: 70 to 100 percent. Dr. Moffett must have rated you mild to moderate. You got the top rating based on his assessment."

"How do I get a higher rating?"

"What do you think you deserve?"

"One hundred percent."

It looked she was going to bust a gut.

"First off, getting 100 percent is very difficult. You really have to be very sick. I've never seen a claim for 100 percent approved without the veteran going to the inpatient treatment program in Canandaigua."

"What's that?"

"It's an intensive program where you're immersed in therapy. It's a group setting with a team of mental health professionals. There are two programs: one is two weeks long and the other is a month long."

"I have to be bad enough to be recommended for one of these programs by my doctor?"

"Yes. The second thing that's missing is you have no history of treatment. My suggestion is cool your jets for a while. Sign up for group sessions; let your doctors and therapists get to know you better; build your medical record. Then resubmit your claim."

By now I had calmed down. I didn't like her answers, but they made intuitive sense to me. I still felt like she was working for the government and not me. I left the MOPH office feeling frustrated with the system. I wanted to know what Dr. Moffett had written in my notes so I filed a request for release of my medical records. When they came, I learned that on the basis of that first appointment, he rated me with a mild to moderate case of PTSD. I was pissed. Blodgett was right, but I still had a feeling in my gut that she didn't have all the facts straight about basic requirements for claims filing. I knew then what I needed to do. I would spend the next 10 months studying the VA's rules and regulations and build my file in preparation for war.

VA Disability Compensation

The MOPH meeting put me in a foul mood. It was two in the afternoon and I was thinking about drowning my sorrows in a cold beer, when David called.

"Heard anything from Compensation and Pension on your claim?"

"Yeah, it came a few days go. It says that I have a mild case and they awarded me a 30-percent rating."

"That's bullshit. If anyone has a strong case, it's you."

"Yeah, tell that to the government; they're there to help the veteran."

"Hey, man, there's no question you were in combat; you've received VA compensation for what, almost 36 years? Plus you were a Green Beret medic, and the claims rate for us is significantly higher than the general soldier population. Think about our mission, man: we were always in the enemy's face."

"Yeah, but I hate this bureaucratic bullshit. How many times do I have to beg in front of the high tribunal to get what I need? I can't work. I can't face the few clients I have left. I'm an emotional wreck. I used the MOPH to file my claim. Well, when I got the news from the VA, I went down there and got real nasty with them; they're supposed to know the system. Nurse Ratched told me I had to go to an inpatient counseling program before the VA would even consider a claim for a hundred percent."

"It's up to your shrink to set the stage for your claim. You need help, man. Call him right now and get in to see him. You need counseling and medication."

I was in Moffett's office the next afternoon. He could see that my condition had worsened. I was shaking with nervous energy. I hadn't shaved in a few days, and must have looked like I hadn't slept well, either. My face was drawn, and I walked with an old man's shuffle.

"Doc, I'm at the state fair last summer and I hear a chopper fly overhead, and I freak-out. Renee and I are sitting in the bleachers at Chevy Court waiting for the Motown Review to come on, and I dive under the seat waiting for a bomb to go off. Crowds didn't bother me before, but now I look for suspicious individuals, particularly Asians, or someone carrying a backpack or satchel, and I cross the street. Loud noises frighten me. If I hear a dumpster lid slam, I jump out of my skin. I'm having nightmares almost every night. Flashbacks are happening all the time. I'm going crazy. I'm out of my mind, out of control. Yesterday, I was driving my car on 690 listening to the Mamas and the Papas, grooving along in the passing lane; I'm doing 80 and my car is ready to jump the bumper of the guy in front. I'm always angry, on edge. What the fuck is happening to me? What am I going to do? I can't work like this; I can't live like this."

Moffett was calm and collected. "We talked about this in our last meeting. I can give you medication for depression, or to take the edge off your anger, or to help you sleep, but there is no drug that will take away all the symptoms."

"What am I going to do? Is a drug-induced coma the only answer?"

"It's a combination of therapies—medication plus counseling. It's all about managing the symptoms. They'll never go away. It's up to you to decide how to react to them. You can work at it, or you can ignore them and become a slave to them. It's up to you."

"Doc, I don't know where to start. I need help; please help me," and I burst into tears.

He let me vent and then reached over with a box of Kleenex and handed them to me. I wiped the tears out of my eyes and off my face, and looked up at him, shaking, feeling like a helpless child.

We practiced the deep-breathing exercise, and he prescribed Celexa and Ambien. It would take a couple of weeks before I noticed any effects from the Celexa. The group meetings hadn't started. He made an appointment for 90 days out. I left his office confused and feeling abandoned.

I considered a civilian shrink, but then discounted it because I had no health insurance, nor money to pay for it. Anyway, I was resigned to build my case within the VA healthcare system for more disability comp. Otherwise, I was fucked.

I couldn't work with my clients anymore. Flashbacks during business meetings were a fact of life. What's a client to think? I had no control over when they'd happen. I was easily distracted because I had sleep apnea, exacerbated by the nightmares. The only way I could retire financially was to have a rating of 100 percent. The possible ratings for PTSD were 30, 50, 70 or 100, based on analyzing the requirements for each published in the VA's compensation tables. Using the byzantine VA compensation formula, a rating of less than 100 for PTSD would make it almost impossible to get to 100 percent total rating without having multiple large disability claims. For instance, my original comp rate in 1969 was 40 percent for physical war wounds. When I was rated for Agent Orange diabetes at 20 percent in 2002, my combined rate went to 50, not 60 percent. The VA formula takes the largest rate as the base, 40 percent in my case, and subtracts that from 100 percent, yielding 60 percent, which forms the basis for calculating the value of the next largest claim. Twenty percent for Agent Orange multiplied by 60 percent equals 12 percent; add that to 40 percent and the result is 52 percent, rounded to the nearest ten. Had the formula come out at 55 percent, my rate would have been 60 percent, and so on.

Moffett rated my PTSD moderate-to-severe after my second session with him, but I questioned whether it would result in a 100-percent claim. I knew I was in bad shape, but I didn't think I was as bad as Ronald or David, both at 100 percent, and some of the guys I'd met at the VA Hospital, who were basket cases. It was possible that I'd get a 70-percent rating. Running the calculations including diabetic neuropathy would bring my overall rating to 90 percent. The difference between 90 and 100 in terms of money and services is significant, roughly 50 percent greater, an additional $1,000 per month, plus full dental coverage, health insurance, and educational benefits for my wife.

The only way I could get to 100 percent was to file for Individual Unemployability. As the name implies, it is designed for vets who, because of their condition, are unable to maintain gainful employment. My consulting jobs paid barely subsistence-level wages. Earnings on my tax returns for the years since being fired from my last employer in 1999 were well below the federal poverty level. It looked like I fit into the IU category.

In November 2006, I filed the revised claim for PTSD, two claims for diabetic neuropathy, and a claim for Individual Unemployability. Blodgett argued that the VA would never approve IU. She was indignant, and it really pissed me off. I had studied the VA rules and regs it uses to adjudicate claims: Title 38 of the Code of Federal Regulations.

"Mr. McShane, the basis for an IU claim is that the veteran must be at a minimum 70-percent rating. What is your rating now?"

"Fifty percent."

"There you go. You're wasting your time and mine," she said smugly.

I collected my thoughts, struggling to keep my cool.

"Ms. Blodgett, Title 38 does, indeed, require that the veteran be comped at a 70-percent rate in order to be considered for IU. However, there are exceptions to the rule. And I quote: 'It is the established policy of the Department of Veterans Affairs that all veterans who are unable to secure and follow a substantially gainful occupation by reason of service-connected disabilities shall be rated totally disabled.' Gainful employment is defined as income at or above the federal poverty level for one person."

She stood standing with her lips pursed and arms folded across her massive bosom.

"Like what, Mr. McShane?"

"Like the last six years as a consultant I've earned less than the federal poverty level." I handed her the four-page essay I intended to attach to the claim filing. It detailed every job and consulting gig I had had since graduating from college in 1973. She glanced at it for a few seconds, and handed it back to me, squinting at me over her reading glasses.

"We've never filed four claims at once, and why are you filing for PTSD again?"

"My PTSD has worsened. I've had several sessions with Dr. Moffett, and I'm in group therapy and seeing Dr. Walden, the psychologist. Moffett has rated me moderate-to-severe. I figure that even if my rating only goes to 50 percent, my combined will go to 80 percent. I think I have a good chance for IU. Obviously, the four claims should be considered together because, under the circumstances, it's clear that I'm not employable in any gainful occupation. Consulting isn't an occupation. It's what you do when you're out of work."

Blodgett was miffed. She didn't often lose an argument, but she couldn't argue with the logic, and she knew that I was right about Title 38.

"Okay, suit yourself, but I'm not optimistic. If you want to file all four claims, go right ahead. I'll have one of my service officers fill out the forms."

Five months later, I received the award letter from the VA with their rating decision: 70 percent for PTSD and 10 percent each for diabetic neuropathy, for a combined rating of 90 percent. Individual Unemployability brought me to 100 percent.

When I went down to the MOPH office to meet with my service officer to explain the benefits available, Blodgett acknowledged my win, and congratulated me. I didn't look at it as a win. I was pissed that I had to become a "compensation lawyer" in order to get what I deserved.

After the award letter came, I applied for Social Security Disability. Within a year, I was receiving checks. I could now pay my bills and together with my wife's income, we could live a modest lifestyle.

VA Counseling

It was November 2005 and Doctor Walden's group had just started, whose purpose was to educate us about PTSD, its symptoms, and manner of treatment. We met every week for six weeks, and I began meeting with her individually. I found her to be less perfunctory than Moffett and more sympathetic to my needs. Following the six weeks, she put me in one of her permanent groups, and I attended that one for the better part of a year, up until the time she moved out of state in September of 2006. She wanted to be near her daughter and two grandchildren in Cleveland, Ohio. I felt a sense of loss because we had gotten to know each other well, and our counseling sessions were helpful.

The group meetings were wasted talking about sports or the weather or other things unrelated to our PTSD. Walden did her best to facilitate our meetings, but it was a difficult task, given that no one in the group wanted to talk about their PTSD except me.

In March, she told me about a creative writing seminar one of the clinical social workers was about to offer, a test balloon to see if there might be a basis for using expressive writing as a treatment modality. The social worker's name was Jan Seeger, and she had a master of fine arts in creative writing. I had just started taking a writing workshop offered by the local YMCA's Downtown Writers Center, having seen a poster on the bulletin board next to the gym locker room. I wanted to share what I had written and get some ideas on how to improve it. The essay I had written after the reunion was dry and boring. Seeger's program was a 12-week introduction to the basics of creative writing: the difference between scene and summary, exposition and setting, character development, narrative forms, and the like. It was fascinating, but the program would not be expanded, or repeated.

Within a few weeks of Dr. Walden announcing her departure, all of her patients were transferred to the existing staff, and her position was not replaced. Jan asked me if I wanted to continue with her as my therapist, and I agreed.

Walden's group dissipated after she left, and I met with Jan, when in mid-2007, she asked if I had an interest in a new program called Cognitive Behavioral Therapy. The idea was to objectify painful memories by going over them in detail in a group setting, and getting feedback.

There were eight in our group, all combat vets. We were asked to identify our most painful memories, and prioritize them. The next step was to articulate the worst memory in writing, and bring it to our second meeting the following week. We would then read it out loud to the group and solicit feedback. My most painful memory was the firefight during which I was wounded. It was difficult trying to remember how I felt during the chaos of the battle, especially since we were trained to focus on the mission, shutting out emotions. I tried to understand why Perez had all of a sudden run straight into the line of fire. While I had only been in country five months, I had been in other firefights, and the first thing we did was hit the dirt for cover and determine how to deploy our strikers. I had never been on an operation with Perez before, so I had no idea what to expect. Because he was our acting company commander while our CO was on R&R, I gave him the benefit of the doubt. We got hit simultaneously. I felt like I had hesitated to go after him, because Sergeant Stevens had to tell me to go get him. When I got hit, I thought it was my fault—I had followed Perez instinctively. But as I wrote down my recollections, I began to think that Perez was at fault, that maybe he was grandstanding, perhaps for a Combat Infantryman Badge, or a medal. These awards were the stock in trade for officers looking for promotion. I began to seethe with anger as I thought about this, but still, after almost 40 years, I questioned myself, taking the blame for my injury. Was I right or wrong in my assessment? All I knew was that I was riddled with guilt, not only for failing to take the initiative myself to go after him, but because I chose not to go back to my team. I decided to save my own ass and go home. I thought I let my team down, that I hadn't given my all, that I was a complete failure, not deserving of the Green Beret I wore.

I read and reread the piece out loud daily before our next session. I had trouble believing what I heard. Then the day came to read it in front of the group. We sat in a circle facing one another and I began.

> Peter McShane 10/1/07
>
> CPT Session 1 Homework
>
> When I got hit, all I could think about was how green I was. My teammates were all seasoned fighters, with an average of two tours; I had five months in country. I was scared to death. My company commander and I had been hit at about the same time, and he was screaming for a medic. I was trying to figure out what to do, tend my own wound, or tend his. One of the sergeants yelled at me to

go up and tend to the captain. When I told him I had been hit, he said, “Shit, and I was just getting to like you.”

I felt like a coward at that point, because I hesitated to respond immediately. I subsequently tended to him and 15 other casualties with the help of one of my Cambodian medics, despite the fact that I had a sucking chest wound. Following this, both the captain and I were extracted from the hot LZ in McGuire rigs. Swinging 60 feet below a chopper flying at treetop level, I watched in horror at muzzle flashes from the jungle canopy below, the NVA trying to finish me off. I waited for the final bullet to put me out of my misery. I was totally helpless and consumed with fear.

This was one of many experiences from the war that has impacted my life. It was my fault that I got hit. I wasn’t attentive enough and should have anticipated a firefight. I feel like a coward, someone who doesn’t have what it takes. As Special Forces medics, we were taught to be no-holds-barred killers, yet compassionate healers. I feel guilt and shame for not having gone back to my team, for abandoning my teammates at a time when medics were in very short supply (for the obvious reason). I was the last of four medics. I feel guilt for having left my dispensary, where we cared for over 2,500 mercenaries and their families. I feel unsafe in crowds, and don’t trust anyone. I don’t feel an emotional bond with my loved ones. I surround myself with activities/projects that ensure that I have no time to think about what happened to me, and what effect my experiences have had on my life. When I do focus on those experiences, they are very painful, but elucidating.

I now know why I aborted my career multiple times: my inability to work for people I neither trusted nor respected. As a result, I have been self-employed most of my working life, in marginal, part-time work. I have experienced significant financial success and the depths of financial failure (bankruptcy). My relationships with others are superficial, at best. I'm divorced. I have no friends, except for a few classmates from Special Forces training who are still alive; they are the only people I can trust implicitly.

AFTER FINISHING, JAN ASKED for feedback from the group.

The first guy to respond was Ed, an infantryman with the 173rd Airborne, a fellow paratrooper. He had been wounded, and was suffering from PTSD, as well.

"Jesus, Pete, you're too hard on yourself. If you ask me, you were a freaking hero for saving your CO. And, by the way, you don't owe your team anything, man."

We went around the room, and everyone else chimed in, incredulous that I took the blame for everything I thought I had done wrong. They each tried to help me put a positive spin on the issues I listed.

"Okay, then what about when I was swinging below the chopper and the gooks were shooting at me. I was scared shitless. I was hoping that they'd shoot Perez and not me."

"Yeah, man, but they didn't. Hey, you beat the odds, McShane. Those fuckers can't hit the broad side of a barn." Laughter erupted.

"Why do you think Perez ran up into the shooting like he did?" asked Marty, a marine who had been stationed in Da Nang.

"I thought he knew something I didn't, plus, he was an officer, so I followed him."

"Do you think he was as green as you?"

I had to think about that. I had assumed that he was seasoned, like Lauder, but maybe not. In five months, I had only seen him on one of our operations, and he wasn't in the field, but in base camp. Could he have been a desk jockey, a wannabe?

"I didn't think so. I thought he was seasoned, but maybe I was wrong."

"Good work, Pete," said Jan. "That must have been difficult."

"It was, but now that I've read it, I feel better, like I've been exonerated. Like maybe, just maybe, I might have done something right."

"That's the idea. Objectifying the experience helps to take the guilt out. You've shared your pain, your burden with other human beings, and they've given you feedback. It's okay to be human."

"Ed, you're next up."

This is the way the group meetings went. Everyone was supposed to come clean, and we would help to objectify the experience. Problem was that not everyone came clean. And when it came to specifying the experience, guys would only talk generally. When we'd try to help them dig deeper, there would be resistance. Then, one by one, they dropped out of the group. By week nine, I was the only one left. I often wondered why; was it a measure of the severity of the experience, or willingness to face pain and defang the memory?

Little Pine Creek Club

I never considered hunting until after the service. As a kid, I knocked over tin cans with my .22 but never went after animals. Bob Turnbull, a friend from Sandy Pond and a champion New York State archer, got me interested in bow-hunting. About my age, he was thick set and funny as hell once he had a few Tanqueray and tonics. At his invitation, I joined a weekly archery league my first semester back at SU, and practiced every day before bow season. It was the only respite I had during that tumultuous spring on campus. We hunted down in the Southern Tier on state land. I'd been down there the previous summer hiking in the pristine forest, having taken a weekend break from rehab at St. Albans Hospital. It reminded me of Uwharrie National Forest, except on a smaller scale. I lost myself in the majesty of the landscape. Bordered by apple orchards and cornfields, it was good habitat for white-tailed deer. Hunting there appealed to me. I was back playing war games at Bragg—it was just me and the enemy. I felt powerful and in control.

I bought a Browning recurve hunting bow, compact but powerful enough to drive a razor-tipped aluminum shaft clear through a deer at 30 yards. I shot bare-bow, with no sight, instinctive shooting the way Native American Indians had hunted. It leveled the playing field. I'd paint up my face in camo, put on my fatigues, and stalk deer. The first time out on a wet and miserable October day, I nailed a buck. Turnbull couldn't believe it; he had bow hunted for five years but never bagged one. I sensed where the deer were and I was patient. I'd wait for them to make a mistake, then they were mine.

Initially, it was the adrenaline rush of pursuit and kill, but communion followed—total and complete domination of my prey. I found curious satisfaction in eviscerating the animals. Once I slit the belly open, intestines spilled onto the forest floor like a steaming plate of pasta. The metallic smell of blood left that familiar taste in my mouth. I'd palpate the piping hot organs in the abdominal cavity for the esophagus, trachea, heart, and bladder, which needed to be carefully cut and removed. Then I'd drag the animal to my truck. After hanging the carcass from a tree limb in the back yard for several days to drain any remaining blood and allow the meat to age, I'd butcher it.

I continued to bowhunt for several years but was having trouble with repeated shoulder injuries suffered in karate, racquetball, and downhill skiing. I didn't have the strength to pull and hold an arrow at full draw for any length of time, and switched to a sight-less compound bow that offered a 30 percent let-off in draw weight, but it was only a question of time before I couldn't handle that, either. Finally, after tearing both rotator cuffs, I was finished bowhunting.

A friend named Tremont belonged to an Adirondack hunting camp and he invited me up once a year for a weekend gun hunt. Little Pine Creek Club was situated on 2,000 acres of prime woodland loaded with maple, walnut, and cherry. The camp building was recent, built in the early 1970s, with a massive stone fireplace, generator, full kitchen, hot and cold running water, full bathroom with shower, bar, and a bunk house off from the kitchen. The terrain was challenging, with rolling hills and deep gullies that flooded during heavy rain. Logging trails crisscrossed the parcel, allowing members to use a truck to ride to any of a dozen hunting locations, which were all mapped. You'd have to be an imbecile to get lost there, but every season a guest would do just that. Two streams ran through the property and it was bordered on one side by a massive state park, and on the other three by private hunting camps. The club was two miles off the paved highway on a gated graveled road that ran through the forest from Brantingham Lake to Stillwater. Ten camps were on that road, including Little Pine Creek. The club had 17 members, not all active, but weekends we'd have 15 to 20 guys prowling the grounds. It was basically a social club, and members were selective about who they'd invite up for a weekend. The members were experienced hunters and it was a family affair with several grandfather, father, and son teams. It was a great place to introduce a boy into the hunting ritual.

It took me almost 20 years, until 1997, before I was offered a membership. I felt honored and especially excited about the prospect of bringing my sons up to mingle with the members and learn how to hunt without having to worry about being shot by some careless jerk. I felt a kinship of sorts with the members and expected friendships to grow. Perhaps I was in search of the same comradeship I had in Special Forces, but it never materialized. I never felt the same closeness or level of trust. They were decent men, and we had lots of laughs, but I didn't like how we hunted. It wasn't challenging. In fact, there was no challenge to it at all. The hunting was done in drives: half of us would be stationed on a watch, while the other half would drive deer to the watchers. It wasn't sportsmanlike, but it was a way to get out in the woods and get some exercise. Some of us hunted alone from tree stands, and a few guys bowhunted, but the majority of the members weren't as adventurous. There were members in their 70s and 80s who still hunted, and the watch-and-drive method was the only way that they would see any hunting action. The younger guys took care of the old guys in the field, made sure they were given a good watch in return for the training they had received as youngsters. From that standpoint, I liked the club, because I could see myself growing old with my sons.

Keith liked the outdoors but never developed an interest in hunting. I had taken him bowhunting once when he was a teenager on a cold and rainy day. We stood for hours waiting for deer to move. He was wet and miserable, and quickly lost interest. Rich tried it a few times, but he, too, had other interests and never got into it. It was Ben who loved to hunt. His first time out, he nailed a six-point buck. He was on a watch across a ravine from me, and I heard five quick shots from his .30 caliber lever action Winchester, the same gun Chuck Connors, "The Rifleman", used, which he'd shoot from the hip. Ten minutes later, I helped Ben track down his buck. I often look at the photo of him and me standing next to his buck, hanging on the buck pole at camp. That evening at the camp bar, we congratulated Ben for his good fortune that day, and he got the nickname The Rifleman from then on. The members loved Ben and it made me proud, but I never felt one with the members. Maybe I was just asking too much of their friendship.

A year after the PTSD diagnosis, I was hunting with some friends and we were driving private land south of Fabius. I was on watch, standing behind several windfalls, and saw a large doe come into range. She was in her prime, maybe two or three years old, probably a mother twice over. As she browsed at the base of a cherry tree for star moss, I put the "V" of my open rear sight on her ribcage just behind the shoulders, lined it up with the bead at the end of the barrel, hesitated for a second, and gently squeezed the trigger. She dropped in a heap. I thought it was a good shot, only about 30 yards. I stood still for a few moments so as not to spook her, listening for any movement, but all I heard was the faint cry of a baby. I thought I was dreaming, that I wasn't really hearing this, that my mind was playing a trick on me, but the doe wailed on, and what came to mind was the thought of my own children, hungry or wet and in distress, a Cambodian child crying in my dispensary, a Vietnamese child crying for the attention of a dead parent. At that moment, I didn't know what to do—finish her off, or try to save her. The faces of wounded strikers flashed through my mind, the ones I couldn't help because it was against orders. I'd watch them bleed to death. I played God. I was their judge and jury. They were guilty of helping us drive the commies out of their own homes. I was guilty of murder, of turning my back on another human being. I had to do something.

I moved in to get a closer look at her wound and she panicked. Lifting her head off the ground, I saw fright in her eyes, the enemy staring her down with a 12-gauge shotgun. She struggled to get up but fell back on her haunches. The slug had entered her abdominal cavity just beneath the diaphragm, which meant that it could be hours before she bled out. I had to finish the job. As I moved closer, she squirmed and tried to get up on her haunches again. I had to put her out of her misery. I put a slug into her chest, and she went down, but she wasn't dead. Wailing, I pulled out my knife to slit her throat, but thought the better of it. I was shaking now, despondent over what I had done, but I knew the only humane thing to do was to kill her. I was about 10 feet from her and as she craned her head toward me again, I fired slug after slug into her chest but she wouldn't die. It was like a slow-motion scene during a firefight. I ran out of ammo, and she was still breathing. I set my shotgun against the cherry tree, and sat with my back against the tree and watched her chest rise and fall for a few minutes until she took her last breath. The heat from her body escaped into the atmosphere, giving rise to wisps of vapor in the cold morning air.

I put my hand on her head. Her eyes were open, an eternal stare for me to remember. Her tongue was flaccid and emerged from between her teeth, much like the onset of death in humans. I took a deep breath and thanked God that it was over.

"I'm sorry. I'm sorry."

I couldn't move. I was catatonic. It took me another half an hour to come to my senses before I gutted and dragged her to my truck. I never took any game without the express intent of consuming the meat, and this doe was no exception, except that she was the last deer I would ever kill.

After that, I looked differently at hunting. I realized that I never enjoyed the killing part. I'd shake in nervous anticipation, adrenaline coursing through my body, hesitate before releasing the arrow or squeezing the trigger. I remembered what Andy Olsen, the sales manager in my father's office, had said about my dad not having the killer instinct. I didn't have the killer instinct either, the thing I thought would make me feel like a man. I began to think about Little Pine Creek and the way that we drove deer, unfairly trapping them in the panic of flight. It wasn't a fair fight. Using a gun wasn't fair. I had stopped hunting fairly when I put down my bow. But there was more to it. I was conflicted.

The week after the incident with the doe, I had one of my VA group meetings at the behavioral health center and I told the guys how I felt about shooting that doe, and that I really didn't want to hunt anymore. I told them about the camp, that I never really felt like I belonged, but I didn't want to let the members down by quitting.

"Who are these guys, and what do you owe them?"

I scanned their faces and tried to think of an answer. I shrugged my shoulders.

"I don't know."

"Are they your buddies?"

I had to think about that, too. They were friends, but after hunting season, we went our separate ways. The camaraderie was short lived.

"I suppose not."

"Why else would you want to stay?"

Ben was the only reason, and he was now married with children and had demands on his time. He seldom went up to camp with me.

"There is no other reason."

"Then follow your heart, man."

That I did. I resigned. The members didn't understand why. There were only three vets in the club, and I told one of them I had PTSD, and that I didn't want to hunt anymore. He was a WWII vet and I don't think he understood.

While the adrenaline rush was part of the lure of hunting, I learned in therapy that hunting was a reaction to the helplessness I felt in the jungles of Vietnam, being hunted by a worthy enemy, out of control, afraid for my life. Back home, I went out in the woods looking for the enemy. I was the one in control.

Jo

My relationship with Jo after the divorce was strained, transient, and skeptical. Being friends was out of the question. The only time we talked was when there was an issue with one of our sons. Our telephone conversations were like the kind you have with a stranger—she was on the defensive. Jo didn't trust me.

I was having lunch with my son Keith in March 2005, several months before the phone conversations with Ronald and David, and he told me that Jo had been diagnosed with cancer. She'd had problems with uterine fibroids when we were still together. After the divorce, she had a partial hysterectomy, but apparently the cancer had already spread and now totally involved her uterus. The tumor was too large to operate and the plan was to try and shrink it first with six months of chemotherapy.

Keith was his mother's man. He did the things around the house that I used to; fixed the leaky faucets, installed new light fixtures, and now took care of her in sickness. Asking him questions about her made me feel like an interloper. I sensed his reluctance to tell me what was going on, as if I had no right to the explanation.

I wanted desperately to be with my sons, to spend more time with them, but I didn't want to trample their relationship with their mother. They were her life, and they confided in her. That's how I always found out about their lives, through Jo. I was the family Green Beret, the one who didn't show emotions, but ironically the emotional parent; she was the tough one. Rich was living with me and going to the community college. Of the three, he was the most like Jo, but they got on each other's nerves. Ben still lived with her. Keith was living with his girlfriend.

In May, I had been reading a book written by a Catholic priest, the rector of our Cathedral. He had been fighting a rare form of cancer that came and went, probably the worst kind. It would go into remission, but never really go away. He had written about his disease with such poignancy that I thought about Jo and decided to send her a copy. I enclosed a mass card along with a short note and sent it off to her. A few days later, she called to thank me for the book. She was surprisingly upbeat. We had a 20-minute conversation about her cancer, other books she had read, her concerns about the chemotherapy, and her work. The tone of our conversation was different than others. Gone was the feeling of distance. I sensed fear and submission, but openness, and hope. Her sister Janet had died of cancer at the age of 50. Jo would be 57 in June.

Over the course of the next six months, the news from the oncologist was encouraging. The tumor was shrinking. In August, after I had been diagnosed with PTSD, I was consumed with guilt after realizing that my behavior toward her was a function of my wartime experiences. I had shut her out physically and emotionally. My work history led to our financial problems and I blamed myself for our lack of security. I sent her a letter of apology.

Dear Jo:

The boys told me about your latest medical hurdle. I hope that by the time you read this, you are resting comfortably at home. I can't imagine how difficult this journey has been for you. I can only say that you have shown great courage and strength as you face this terrible illness. As I look back on our years together, there were many happy times we shared, punctuated by behavior on my part that I now recognize as hurtful and insensitive.

Over the last three months, I have faced the demons of my past in Vietnam. Nightmares and flashbacks have come after me since talking with some of my medic classmates. As they told me about the problems in their lives, I realized that my behaviors over the last 36 years were all classic signs of posttraumatic stress disorder: inability to get close to others; lack of trust; guilt; anger. I pushed my loved ones away—pushed you away.

I am under the care of a VA *psychiatrist. With his help, I hope to understand what these demons are and how to cope with them. Nevertheless, I'll be living with the memories of my past actions for the rest of my life.*

I'm not asking for your sympathy, but rather begging your forgiveness for the things I may have said or done to hurt you.

I wish you a speedy recovery. My prayers are with you.

Love,

Pete

In November, two months after my reunion, surgeons went in to remove her diseased uterus, only to find that the cancer had spread throughout her abdomen—stage 4. The doctors gave her one, maybe two months to live. When Keith called to tell me, I was shocked. I guess I understood the downside risk, but I didn't want to believe it. I hung the phone up and began to cry, deeply. All I could think of at the time was the young woman who had rescued me from myself back at Fort Devens. I couldn't rescue her. I was despondent. I felt like I needed to do something, but I didn't know what. I had been attending noon Mass daily after the first news of Jo's cancer, in hopes of feeling some relief, but the pangs of guilt wouldn't go away. Instead, they got worse. Toward the end of the service, the day after Keith called, when the priest stood before the congregation and proclaimed, "peace be with you", I knew I had to see Jo, to talk with her. I ran out of church.

As I drove up to the hospital, my mind drifted. I had a mental image of Jo as a beautiful, healthy young woman with our sons when they were young, but I knew she wouldn't look like that. I had seen her over the summer when I helped Keith move to a new home. He had stored some furniture in Jo's basement. She had already undergone three rounds of chemo, and she looked tired. Her body was bloated, puffy. She had lost her hair and was wearing a shorthaired wig that was the wrong color for her jaundiced skin.

I tried to prepare myself for the worst. I walked into her room and she was sitting up in her bed, one day after surgery. She looked up, smiled, and in a surprised but pleasant tone said, "Hi, Pete".

"Hi, Jo." I stood there in the doorway and didn't know what to do next, turn and run out of the door, or walk over to the bed.

A nun was in the room visiting her, and Jo immediately introduced me as her former husband.

"Come over here, next to my bed," as she held out her hand.

I sat on the side of the bed next to her, and she took my hand in hers. For a moment, I could feel a wave of emotion rising in me. I took a deep breath. The nun was saying some prayers over Jo, and, as the nun placed her hands on Jo's head, it dropped to the nun's bosom. I could see the tears running down Jo's cheek. The nun turned to bid me farewell, took Jo's hands in hers and said "God bless you, my dear". As the nun walked out the door, Jo looked over at me, the tears still welling in her eyes.

"Keith told me, Jo. I am so sorry. I … I wish there was something I could do."

She looked up at me, and at that precise moment, I leaned in, hugged her, and burst into tears. We cried together for what must have been five minutes. I could feel years of frustration and pain flow out of my body as I held her close to me. I was trembling, and I know she could feel it. She held me tight; I sensed her fear.

"I can't believe this is happening. How am I going to carry on without you? How am I going to fill your shoes; you're so involved in the boy's lives."

Our sons were her life. Now we had four grandkids and they were an integral part of her life, too. I was on the periphery up until now, choosing not to compete with her for their affection. They were all she had.

Sobbing, she said, "Pete, it's the little things that count. Just be there for them."

She looked up at me, tears streaming down her cheek, "Let bygones be bygones, okay?"

At that moment, I felt a strange sense of relief, vindication of sorts. The strain in our relationship since our divorce washed away with those tears. At least now, maybe we could be friends for the time that she had left.

The doctors told her that she would need weekly dialysis because her kidneys had shut down. Faced with prolonging the inevitable, she refused treatment, and decided instead to go home. The doctors said that as toxins built up in her body, she would slowly slip away into a coma and die peacefully; it would take days, perhaps a week or two. Hospice nurses visited her daily and made sure that she was comfortable. Her appetite was weak, and the jaundice got worse by the day. People would ask, "How's she doing?" knowing well enough that she was dying and there would be no reversal.

Our sons were there on the front lines. They literally camped out. Rich, who lived in New York City, quit his job. I felt like I needed to be there, too. I visited her almost every day. It was an amazing time for me, painful but liberating. We were a family again, if only for a few weeks. Renee was wonderful and understanding during this difficult time. She truly loved me and knew that I needed to be a part of Jo's end-of-life ceremony.

The calendar marked time. My sons and I maintained a constant vigil, to the point that Jo would get upset with us for making her feel closed-in. Jo's sister and her kids, nephews, cousins, and childhood friends were part of this. For those few short weeks, it was like we had never been separated. Mutual friends who disappear when a couple divorces became friends again, if only for the ceremony. We were all waiting for her to die.

Jo asked me to write her obituary. We went over it several times before she was satisfied with it. She also wanted me to say something at the funeral, as I had when Dale, her father, had passed. I told her I would read it to her after I finished it, but decided not to. It would have been too painful for me; just waiting for her to die was enough to handle.

The constant stream of visitors jammed her tiny home and kept her going, but it left her exhausted and agitated. We didn't want to let her go, and she didn't want to let us down. It was painful to watch. She slept most of the time, but waking hours were filled with visiting and nervous anticipation of things not ready for her passing. During one of these frenzied moments, she gathered up our sons and directed that they take her to the funeral home, where she proceeded to make her own arrangements. She chose the music and the method—she would be cremated. No one in the family wanted her pet boxer Cade, so she agreed to give him to one of her coworkers. She and Rich drove out to the coworker's farm, and when she saw how rundown it looked, they turned around and came home. When Keith heard this, he agreed to take him.

We had impromptu family meetings where she would implore the boys not to fritter away their inheritance, and she asked me to make sure they used the money wisely, even though they were grown men. At her insistence, they cast lots for her furniture, car, and belongings. It embarrassed them. It embarrassed me. These were uncomfortable sessions, and rather than pooh-pooh her requests, we acquiesced and agreed.

Her behavior became more erratic as the toxins built up in her blood stream. This maudlin ordeal continued for five weeks. We hung around her house waiting for her to cry or ask for something or yell at us. We wanted to help her desperately, but there was nothing that anyone could do to make it easier for her to pass.

I GOT THE CALL FROM KEITH early on a Tuesday. It was a sunny day in January, crisp and chilly, the ground lightly covered with fresh snow. Jo had taken her last breath at seven thirty that morning. He and Rich were there by her side when she died. When I pulled up to her house, Keith's wife was coming out, and she came up to me, reached her arms out to embrace me and gave me a big hug.

"I'm so sorry."

"So am I … so am I."

I proceeded to the house, and walked to the side door and into the kitchen. I saw Rich over against the counter by the window, next to the coffee machine. He came over, we hugged, and he began crying.

"It's okay, honey. Mom is in a better place."

I consoled him for a few moments and then Keith walked in from the living room where Jo's bed was stationed. I placed my hands on Rich's shoulders, looked at him affectionately, and turned to embrace Keith. As I put my arms around him, I began to cry and he consoled me.

"It's okay Dad, she didn't suffer. Her breathing was labored all night, and early this morning I could hear her mumbling, trying to say something, but I knew she couldn't. Then she just stopped breathing. Do you want to see her?"

I nodded and turned to walk into the living room. The covers were pulled to her chin. Her mouth was agape, open in a way that you only see in the dead, teeth exposed as if the lips had receded. I bent over to kiss her forehead, her skin still warm. I reached for her arm, and at that moment, fell to my knees and wept into her bosom.

Perez

For years, I believed that I had failed on the Bunard mission, the firefight during which Perez and I got wounded. If I hadn't been following him, I wouldn't have been shot. He could have been grandstanding for a medal, something I'd expect from a young officer, not a seasoned one. Rushing into an enemy position was not SOP on our team, but that's what he did. He could have learned it in one of the basic infantry tactic classes in Officer Candidate School—classic operations where you can see the enemy—WWI, WWII, Korea. It doesn't work in the jungle. You can't see the enemy. You can't see your own men.

Perez was Nigel Lauder's best buddy. Both Cuban exiles, veterans of the failed CIA-led Bay of Pigs invasion. I had great respect for Lauder, our CO, and assumed by association that Perez was a seasoned warrior. He wasn't a member of our team, and I knew my teammates never trusted outsiders, which amounted to anyone they didn't know. Some officers and senior NCOs from headquarters were given a chance to experience the combat environment as part of their education as military leaders, to let them qualify for a Combat Infantryman Badge, or if they got lucky, a medal. They'd go out on "low-risk" operations, maybe a klick or two into the bush, spend a few days tromping through the jungle to experience what it was like being a grunt, then go back to their desks.

I was still green compared to my lifer teammates, and was right behind Perez on that operation. I needed to trust him, so I gave him the benefit of the doubt. Perhaps to bolster my own self-image, I would never have considered a trained Special Forces operative to be incompetent.

In VA counseling, I questioned not only my own performance in Vietnam, but the motives and actions of others. I judged everyone based on my own standards of performance, which my shrink said were impossibly high. I expected the same extraordinary personal commitment from everyone, the same commitment that I expected and received from my Special Forces teammates. There were incompetents everywhere, even Special Forces officers. The stories from David, Ronald, and other medic classmates bore this out. I spent years not wanting to believe or acknowledge this, because it had a direct impact on my own self-esteem. My adult life was forged on my image as a Green Beret. I was angry. I thought that Perez fucked up. I hated him and what his failure might say about me.

One of my classmates at the reunion who had replaced me on the Mike Force had also served with Lauder. Short of interrogating him, I wanted to know if he had heard any scuttlebutt about me. When he said my teammates had nothing but good things to say, I was shocked. I looked around the hotel meeting room and out the window. Yellow haze shrouded the foothills of the Sierras in the distance. I couldn't put the words into context. I never thought I'd get feedback about my performance in Nam. And yet, there it was, dished up like a gourmet meal. I should have felt validated, but I didn't. He gave me Lauder's e-mail address, but I had no interest in making contact. Why push it? At least, it isn't negative feedback. But I had to know.

In 2006 after months of counseling, I got up the courage to send Lauder an e-mail asking about him and Perez. There was a response within 15 minutes:

> Dearest Pete: I am delighted to receive your e-mail and to know that you are doing well. Rico Perez's e-mail is rperez@xyz.com. Please send him an e-mail … he will be delighted to hear from you …. You are a hero in his mind and in mine, too.
>
> I feel sorry that I missed the Bunard operation. I went on R&R to Hawaii to see my sweetheart. We married on November 16, 1968 after I had spinal surgery from a helicopter crash soon after you were wounded.
>
> If you have an opportunity to visit the Washington area, please let me know and we will make room for you and your wife. Yesterday we gave my oldest daughter a wedding at Fort McNair in DC. It was fabulous and we had many grunts in the ceremony.
>
> You are welcome anytime.
>
> De Oppresso Liber, Nigel

I was in shock. Never did I expect a response like that. After 36 years of carrying Perez's crucifix, the definitive judgment came from a man I had held in the highest regard, a man I had followed into battle and trusted with my life. I was elated and overcome with emotion. I sat at my desk crying as I read the e-mail over and over. All the things that the shrinks and counselors had told me about my overcritical self-judgment were true. They had said: "With a bullet hole in your chest, you saved Perez's life, plus the lives of 15 Cambodian strikers. And you think that you didn't do enough?" I realized how absurd it sounded, but it's difficult to change ingrained perceptions.

No sooner than I wiped the tears from my face, the phone rang.

"Pete? This is Rico Perez."

I had often wondered what I would say or do to Perez if we ever met again. I despised the man. I wanted to scream at him, call him a fucking incompetent worthless piece of shit. I trusted you, motherfucker! I thought of all the ways that I could belittle him, perhaps in front of Lauder or his family, make him feel the kind of crushing self-deception I had endured for 36 years at his hands. Yes, I hated myself because of him.

"I am so glad that you contacted Lauder. I often think of you," he said.

Tension filled my gut. Where do I start? Standing in the kitchen, I thought about calling him Captain, but that was 36 years ago, and he'd be a bird colonel by now. But you're a civilian, and he introduced himself as Rico.

He's still a fucking asshole. I held the phone so tight that my hand began to cramp.

"Hello … Rico …" I felt strange calling him by his first name.

He seemed anxious, almost out of breath.

"You saved my life, and I'm grateful. Thank you from the bottom of my heart." The words stuck in my ear, his Spanish accent coloring his voice, charged with emotion. I conjured up an image of the man on the other end of the line—bald and paunchy, tears streaming down his cheeks. He was sobbing.

"I just did my job."

"You did a lot more than your job, my man. You could have let me die … saved your own ass … Hey, did you get your Silver Star?"

My team XO had visited me at the MASH hospital and said he had submitted me for the award. I thought I didn't get it because I had fucked up.

"No. I got a Bronze Star with 'V'."

Perez was livid. He shouted into the phone: "I can't believe that! Those damn pencil necks! I put you in for the Silver Star twice."

Could that be true? How many times can you put a guy in for a medal and still get turned down? I couldn't help thinking that had I been an officer, even one from behind the lines, I would have been awarded the Silver Star. Still in a huff, he said, "Jesus Christ, Pete, you should have gotten the Distinguished Service Cross for what you did." He floored me. The DSC is second only to the Congressional Medal of Honor. Holy shit! Medals were the stuff of military careers. I wanted that Silver Star as validation of a job well done —but it never came. As far as I was concerned, I had fucked up. And every time I'd think of how Perez kept yelling for a medic, that he didn't even know my name, it made me feel like a worthless piece of shit. Now, it meant little more than a reminder of how close I came to dying for someone else's mistake.

"How you doing, I mean, with your wounds?" he said.

I really didn't want to talk about it, but I had to say something.

"I took an AK round in the chest. Luckily you and I got to the MASH in time for surgery. I had two surgeries and after ten days in recovery, I was shipped to Camp Zama, Japan, for observation. From there I spent five months recuperating stateside in the hospital." I didn't say anything about PTSD.

"How about you?"

"My gut wounds got infected and took a while to heal. My arm was really fucked up. Two years of physical therapy and it's still not right. Luckily I was able to go back to active duty with SF."

Perez said he did another tour in 1972 with SOG, running covert ops into Laos, and then went on to other assignments. I thought about how crazy you'd have to be to go back into battle after getting shot up like we were. You've got to be addicted to adrenalin, or have a death wish. Was he an incompetent? Maybe like the rest of us, he learned to be a warrior on the job.

"Lauder and I did some state department work, you know CIA. Now we're both pushing 70. Maybe we'll retire someday. Hey, we're neighbors. You're always welcome here, my man. Please come down. I'd love to see you."

I had known the man for little more than a day, and hated him most of my life. Now we're best buddies? I envisioned him hugging me, slobbering on my shoulder, his family pawing me over like some kind of holy savior.

"I'll look you and Nigel up next time I'm in DC."

He signed off.

What could I say? Perez was just a run-of-the-mill career officer who's alive today because a medic did his job, period. Hey, he said thank you. What more could you ask?

MY MIND WAS OVERRUN WITH feelings that I couldn't put into perspective. Thirty-six years of tension dissipated as if someone had stuck me with a pin and let out the pus. I had done my job, a good job. Period. Yet, I should have felt elation and joy. I'd always thought of officers as being somehow superior and deserving of respect. I suppose I could blame my Catholic upbringing. Priests and nuns would say: "Obey your parents, obey your superiors; they know what's good for you." After Perez, I scorned all officers. You'll have to earn my respect. Rank and privilege don't equate to experience, character, and fortitude.

While doing research for this story, I learned that our team had been decimated a month after I was wounded in a vicious battle where many of my teammates died. There's no question I would have been there had I not been medevaced. It occurred to me that Perez may have saved my life.

When searching a database of medals awarded to Special Forces units, I remembered how I felt after receiving the Bronze Star certificate in the mail. I didn't want to know whether Perez had been awarded a medal, because it would have made me feel even worse about my performance. It was inconceivable that he could have received any medal at all, but there it was: Rico Perez was awarded the Silver Star for his actions that day. It confirmed my long-held belief—rank has its privileges.

Daddy, Did You Kill Anybody in Vietnam?

We were visiting Smithsonian museums during the 1988 spring vacation. Keith was 13, Rich was 11, and Ben was a month shy of seven. The weather in DC that week was glorious. The cherry blossoms and warm weather regaled us after a long and snowy winter in Syracuse. We'd had our fill of skiing and a stretch of 70-degree weather was welcome.

The museums were fabulous, but after three days of traipsing through display after display, and covering what seemed like every square foot of the National Mall, the boys were getting bored and fidgety. Jo suggested we spend our final day visiting the National Aquarium, Washington Monument, and the Lincoln Memorial. It was midafternoon by the time we climbed the steps to the top of the Washington Monument, and we were beat. We decided to drive to the Lincoln Memorial rather than walk. Traffic was heavy. We found a parking spot off Constitution Avenue and crossed the street to the Mall. Crowds were thick. We made our way through the Mall following the signs for the Lincoln Memorial, when suddenly ahead of us was "The Wall." Startled, I froze amid the moving crowd. I had seen pictures and video clips, and tried to imagine what it would be like to be there in person, but there was no way I could have predicted its effect on me.

"Dad, Dad … over here!" shouted Keith. The family was 20 yards ahead staring at me suspended in the current of tourists.

"Dad—it's the Vietnam Veterans Memorial!"

A few seconds later, Jo came back to where I was standing.

"Are you okay?"

"Not really. I … I don't think I can deal with this today."

She grabbed my hand. "You know, your sons should see this."

We walked hand-in-hand down the sloping walk adjacent to the polished black granite wall. The mood was somber, a public wake. People wandered trance-like, connecting with the spirits of loved-ones. Men in tattered jungle fatigues sobbed, perhaps trying to come to terms with what they had or hadn't done in Vietnam. I struggled to contain my emotions as I thought how fortunate I was, mourning and not being mourned. My sons stood by me as I searched for names: Andy Stein from Syracuse. I met his mother at graduation from Basic. She had asked me to watch out for him. After that, we were split up. I touched Andy's name, etched into the cold granite.

"Who is it, Dad?" asked Keith.

"A buddy from basic training."

"Is he dead?" asked Ben.

I nodded.

"Let's say a prayer for Andy's soul."

I watched them make the sign of the cross, and holding their hands together in prayer, stood there as if in church, waiting for the priest to say the Funeral Mass was over.

We spent an hour touching names, saying a prayer for a high school friend, a neighbor, and a few Special Forces buddies. The last one was Danny Keyes, a teammate killed in a firefight a month after I was medevaced. I told the boys that he had been shot in the head with a .50 caliber machine gun. We were praying for Danny, when Ben looked up at me.

"Daddy, did you kill anybody in Vietnam?"

"Ben!" Jo shushed him with a wave of her arm.

The boys stood aghast, their younger brother having shattered our prayerful silence. I never talked about my military service, but knew there'd come a day when I'd have to explain myself. I waved my hand and told Jo it was okay.

Memories become distorted over time, and the painful ones are buried in the subconscious. I don't recall firing my weapon during a firefight. I could say that I never knowingly took another person's life, but I didn't want to complicate my answer. There was more to it.

I knelt facing Ben and placed my hands on either shoulder.

"No, I didn't."

There were smiles across the boys' faces, relief.

"That's good," said Rich. "It would have been a mortal sin."

I was a medic, but also an infantryman, and the executive officer of a 125-member company of Cambodian "strikers," mercenaries. I carried an M-16 and a Browning 9mm sidearm and was expected to use them. My primary role in the field was tactical—leading our strikers into battle. Being a medic was only important if one of my teammates was hit. As testament, I was awarded the Combat Infantryman Badge rather than Combat Medic Badge.

Strikers under my command were brutal warriors and killed plenty of the enemy. Does that mean that I killed the enemy? Do I bear responsibility for the lives of prisoners who were tortured and beheaded by my men? They violated the Geneva Convention, the core of international humanitarian law. Does that mean that

I broke the law? I knew it was wrong, and I turned my back, but who was I to object? I was the youngest and least experienced man on our team. My teammates said don't meddle; there's 200 years of bad blood between the Cambodes and the Vietnamese. Does that exonerate me? My orders were not to render lifesaving medical care to the enemy. I watched them die. Am I not to blame? I struggle with these moral questions.

I also struggle with another question: Why didn't I kill the enemy in Vietnam? Was it unwillingness or cowardice? In five months of field duty, I went on close to a dozen operations, six involving a firefight, and the last one almost cost me my life. In Vietnam, the enemy was the jungle; Charlie and the NVA hid there. I never saw the enemy face to face. Who are you shooting at when you shoot in the direction of incoming fire into an opaque wall of green and brown vegetation? In zero visibility, I'd ask myself where are my strikers? They were committed to our ops, but undisciplined and barely competent in rudimentary military tactics. It was just as likely they were hidden in jungle growth in front of me as on my flank. I'd think about where to aim my M-16 and hesitate. In the chaos of a firefight, mistakes happen. Friendly fire accidents are a fact of life, especially with indigenous troops.

Would I have had the guts to take Charlie's life? I never had to prove to myself that I could pull the trigger in a faceoff. But I had the courage under fire to save a teammate's life, and 15 of our strikers, despite having a sucking chest wound. What does that say about me? Nevertheless, the doubts about whether I had what it takes to take another life festered for years, the same doubts I had when a bully threatened me as an adolescent, afraid to take a swing at him. I feared losing control, letting my animal loose. I'd think about how to answer the question that Ben asked, and not want to embarrass myself. It threatened my self-image as a Green Beret. I needed to feel accepted in the brotherhood, and felt that killing the enemy was the gateway to that acceptance.

Ironically, I didn't have to pull the trigger myself to see the enemy's face in my nightmares, to see him beg for his life. I read his love letters, stared at his photos of beautiful young women and children, wondered how his family would take the news of his death. I held a man's rosary beads in my fingers and wondered whether we prayed to the same god. I cried for his soul and prayed for my own.

Sharing the Scourge of War

When I was diagnosed with diabetes in 2001, my uncle, a WWII vet, said that the VA had linked Type 2 diabetes with exposure to Agent Orange, a powerful dioxin used extensively to defoliate the jungle in Vietnam. It was news to me. We routinely sprayed the jungle foliage surrounding our A-Camps, but proving individual exposure was a problem for some veterans, depending on where they were stationed. Frankly, I hadn't paid much attention to news media reports in the '70s and '80s that Vietnam vets blamed Agent Orange for cancers and other horrendous medical conditions and their children's birth defects. The VA steadfastly claimed there was no conclusive scientific evidence of a direct link with Agent Orange exposure, yet several of the manufacturers of Agent Orange settled a product liability and class-action lawsuit in 1984 filed on behalf of men and women who had served in Vietnam. It took another seven years for the passage of the Agent Orange Act of 1991, which set forth the presumption of exposure to all Vietnam era vets. That Act directs the VA to compensate those veterans without the need for proof of exposure. The Act details the many physical ailments caused by Agent Orange, notably Ischemic Heart Disease, certain Leukemias, Multiple Myeloma, Hodgkin's and Non-Hodgkin's Lymphoma, Parkinson's Disease, and Prostate Cancer, among others. Diabetes Mellitus Type 2 was the first to be identified with the others added only as it became obvious there was a connection with Agent Orange. The Agent Orange Benefits Act of 1996 addressed the offspring of poisoned veterans by adding Spina Bifida and associated physical birth defects, but it did not address developmental defects.

While building my case for VA disability compensation in 2006, I perused veterans' Internet forums to help me understand how to deal with the huge bureaucracy. Amid the grousings of vets unhappy with their ratings, there was talk about children with Autism, ADHD, OCD, and Bipolar Disorder. The comments expressed concern that these conditions might be linked to Agent Orange exposure. With further research, I found studies confirming that developmental delays, learning disabilities, and attention deficit and behavioral disorders have indeed been discovered in children and grandchildren of exposed veterans.

Growing up, my three sons displayed evidence of delayed development. My wife and I weren't alarmed at the time because children develop at their own pace. We held our two oldest back in first grade because they needed time to "mature", as the school psychologist said. While our oldest son passed successfully into second grade, our middle child had difficulty grasping tasks and concepts. A battery of tests discovered he had developmental disorders, specifically problems with short-term memory, verbal expression, and social skills. So did our youngest child, but to a lesser extent. Ultimately, both of them received special educational preferences throughout primary and secondary school.

My grandchildren have also experienced developmental problems. One has been diagnosed with Auditory Processing Disorder, and three display some of the same symptoms as their fathers, (i.e., problems with short-term memory, verbal expression, and social skills). It remains to be seen whether my five youngest grandchildren will have similar learning disabilities.

The VA intimates that additional birth defects beyond Spina Bifida may be covered under the Agent Orange Benefits Act, but the defects must have resulted in a permanent physical or mental disability, and it's up to the veteran to prove it.

After having to provide the VA with proof that I was in combat, while war wounds detailed in my VA medical records clearly gave them all the proof they needed to support my claim for compensation, how would I go about proving that my children and grandchildren may have been poisoned by Agent Orange?

Isn't it enough that veterans have been stricken by the scourge of war, but must our families carry that burden as well?

Al

"Al wants to be a marine. Ian and I are sick about it."

It was June 2008, and my sister Alice had called hoping that I might have some words of wisdom for them. My nephew had just graduated from Norwich Military College in Vermont with a BS in civil engineering. He was enrolled in Army ROTC through his sophomore year, but began to waffle when cadre intimated that second lieutenants were expendable on the battlefield. During his junior and senior years, he continued in ROTC but remained uncommitted, toying with the idea of going in the navy. In his senior year, he was offered a civilian job with the army. Now, it was the marines.

"Would you like me to speak with him?"

"Please. Ian and I would be grateful."

"You know how I feel about war. Maybe I can talk some sense into him. Now that he's home from school, I'll invite him out to dinner."

I remember what a pain in the ass Al was as a kid. The youngest of four children, he was interested in the military ever since he was old enough to walk and talk. As a toddler, he played with toy soldiers, and terrorized his two older sisters. He would lie in wait in the bushes in front of their house, hoping to scare the shit out of one or both of them. When he was old enough to read, it was books about the military: uniforms, weapons, and vehicles. At seven, I gave him my Green Beret. He strutted around the house dressed as a soldier, wearing little boy fatigues, a toy M-16, and my Green Beret, so large it sat on either ear. I thought it was a hoot. From that point on, I was his hero. As a preteen, he was an active participant in Civil War reenactments, having been drafted as a drummer boy. During high school, he expressed a desire to go to West Point, but ultimately enrolled at Norwich. It was fitting that I would be the one to try and dissuade him from going into the service.

"Al, its Uncle Pete."

"Hi. How are you?"

"I'm good. When did you get back from school?"

"Last weekend. I'm just settling in and thinking about a summer job. I need to make some money to support my habits." We laughed.

After some idle chitchat, we agreed to meet at Pablo Gallo's, the Mexican restaurant in the village. Alice told me Al had the summer to think about his options. The next Marine Corps OCS class wouldn't start until October. A couple of hours before we were to meet at the restaurant, I prayed for guidance. I didn't know how much Al knew about my situation, but I was prepared to lay it all on the table in hopes of convincing him to take a civilian job, any civilian job.

The restaurant was crowded. It was July third, the evening before the long holiday weekend, probably a poor choice for a quiet talk. We were seated at a table in the bar, busy with people waiting to be seated in the restaurant. Even though Al wasn't my son, I felt a special bond with him, and I hurt inside at the thought that this young man could wind up being another tool of the government and political leaders who had no personal concept of what it was like to go to war.

"It must feel good to be finished with school."

"Yeah. It feels great."

The waiter came over and put menus down, and asked if we cared for a drink.

"I'll have a Dos Equis. Al, what do you want?"

"I'm going to stick with water."

I was curious that he didn't order a beer. I thought that maybe his parents had told him not to drink, or maybe he anticipated the depth of our conversation and wanted to be completely sober when sparring with me. I took a long drag on the bottle and felt the beer bite my throat, and followed with two more. I was tense, unsure of myself and where our conversation might take us.

"What's your plan this summer?"

"Get a job, make some money and figure out what I want to do."

"Thinking about the future is a good idea, Al."

"I've been doing a lot of thinking. Mom and Dad have tried to help me sort the options. I want to have a family, have a good job, have a boat and a nice car like you and my mom and dad." He took a sip of water. "At the end of my sophomore year, I decided against going into the army. All I heard was how second lieutenants were cannon fodder. It scared me."

His comment surprised but encouraged me. I thought that perhaps my job of convincing him might have gotten easier.

"Al, you were raised in a home not unlike the one in which your mother and I were raised. We're sensitive, emotional people, not prone to violence. The service is licensed violence. Young officers are vulnerable in times of war. I could tell you some stories."

Al nodded his head.

The waitress came over and asked if we were ready to order. We hadn't opened the menus.

"Give us a minute," I said.

There was a lull in our conversation while we perused the menus. Al looked almost relieved. He took a couple more sips of his water and shifted in his seat. I waived for the waitress and she took our order. "I decided not to seek a commission in the army, but instead consider other branches of the service. Along the way, the army offered me a job as a civilian engineer at Fort Monmouth, New Jersey. It was a research position, and I want a job as a process engineer, like in a plant."

So why are you even considering the marines? I thought. I could feel the tension built in my gut.

"What happened with the navy?"

"The program included extensive training in nuclear engineering, essentially a graduate engineering degree, paid for by the navy. Unfortunately, my grades were a problem, and they turned me down."

He gestured with his hands, palms up, while his facial expression read disappointment. I took another tug on my beer, steeling myself for what was to come.

"I had heard that you were considering Marine Aviation."

"Yeah, I did. Some of the guys at school have already signed up for the program. They've been walking around campus with flight jackets and sunglasses. I've been talking with a marine recruiter about OCS. The officer training program is three segments, each three months long. Boot Camp is the first; the second involves rotating through all five of the command branches to see which we like the best. You spend three weeks in each area, such as infantry, artillery, logistics, and so forth; the last segment is specific training in your chosen field. The recruiter said that we get a couple of command choices, and they do their best to give us what we want."

Here we go; the propaganda machine, I thought.

"Al, don't believe everything you hear. You know, of course, that in a time of war, when troop strength is low, the marines are going to select infantry for you; you won't have a choice."

He took another sip of his water, and glanced around the bar. The crowd was a distraction, as people jockeyed to order drinks while they waited for tables.

"I know, Uncle Pete. In fact, I want the infantry."

I was in the middle of a drag on my Dos Equis, and choked on it.

"You want to go into the infantry?"

"Yeah."

I struggled to remain composed.

"How does the infantry fit into your long-range plan?"

"I know, it sounds crazy. I've been thinking about this for months. I've read a bunch of leadership books and I want to test my mettle; I want to see if I have what it takes. You did it, Uncle Pete."

Fuck. Now what? I've got to let him have it.

"You're right, Al. I did it. But I'm here to tell you that I made a mistake, a huge mistake."

Al became animated, his torso and arms driving a sales pitch that he had practiced, no doubt on his parents and other disbelievers.

"I've even read memoirs written by veterans who have fought in Iraq and Afghanistan. I just finished a book written by a former marine captain, a company commander. He was frank about the risks, and how difficult it is to reacclimate to civilian life. In fact, he almost didn't get into grad school because the admissions committee didn't think that experience as a soldier was a good enough reason to admit him."

He was trying to paint a balanced picture that being a soldier has its ups and downs, just like any other profession.

"Al, did any of this guy's soldiers get wounded or killed?

"Yes."

"What was his comment on this; what did he have to say?"

"That he would have to live with the painful memories for the rest of his life."

"And even after reading all that, you still want to go in?"

"Yes."

Vibrating with anger, I wanted to reach across the table and throttle him. Thankfully, the waitress brought our meal. We started to eat, but neither one of us dug in. I picked at the food while I tried to figure out how to respond. I knew I couldn't go off on him. I'd surely lose the argument.

"None of us go to war thinking about the downside. Somehow, those thoughts never come up because the testosterone floods our brains and distorts reality. You ought to ask your recruiter how difficult it is to make a life for yourself with legs or arms missing. There is no glory in war, only pain and suffering." I paused for a few seconds. "You knew that I was wounded, didn't you?"

"Yes."

"Well, after the bullet missed my heart by a few millimeters, I thought I was invincible. I strutted around like I was a fucking hero. I used that wound as a badge of courage and hid under the Green Beret for years because I really didn't know who I was. Three years ago, I went to a reunion of guys from my SF Medics class. Out of a class of 56, there were 18 of us there. Some of us were killed in Nam, others committed suicide after; most of us are fucked up. Al, there I was in a room full of broken men, crying over what we had done to other human beings in the war. Do you know that I have PTSD?"

"Yes."

"I am a hundred percent disabled. I can't work anymore. I see a team of shrinks and psychologists every month. I'm in group sessions every week with other Vietnam vets whose lives have been destroyed. I know that you think my life has been good, with the summer homes and the fast cars and boats. But the truth is that I have been running from my wartime experiences since I got out in 1969. I had no career, I have no security, no savings, my marriage blew up, and I've been bankrupt. I'm on a VA pension now and if it wasn't for that, I'd be living in a fucking cardboard box. Life isn't necessarily as simple as it appears on the surface."

Al had leaned back in his chair during my fusillade. He looked like he had taken a direct hit. He was speechless. I was spent. We picked at our food for another ten minutes without saying a word. The cacophony of voices in the bar swallowed us in idle chatter. I'm glad we were out there, rather than sitting at a quiet corner booth. The silence would have been deafening. There was nothing more to say.

The waitress came to clear our table and I paid her. Al and I walked out to the parking lot.

"Uncle Pete, I appreciate that you thought enough of me to have this talk." He extended his hand, and I took it.

"Al, a friend of mine, my therapist at the VA, reminded me of two characters in classic literature. There are two kinds of people in this world: Knights and Merlins. It's taken me years to understand that I've been hiding under my Green Beret because I'm no Knight, never was. I'm a Merlin, an empathetic, emotional, sensitive human being. I'm not a killer and neither are you. Be true to yourself."

AL SHIPPED OUT IN OCTOBER. I felt like I had failed him. Then I thought how my parents must have felt when I enlisted in the army. I know they weren't happy with me, but there was nothing they could have done to change my mind. It had been time for my journey, and now it was time for Al's.

Two months after Al had shipped out to Quantico for OCS, I went to the grocery store one evening and as I parked my car, I saw Al walking toward his car across the aisle from me. I jumped out and yelled his name. I couldn't believe my eyes. We shook hands and I hugged him. He was smiling, but looked like he didn't want to see me.

"What are you doing here, Al?"

He looked down at the pavement for a minute.

"I resigned my commission."

The words hit me in the solar plexus like I had been drop-kicked. It was the last thing I expected to hear. I thought maybe he was home for a few days on leave.

"What happened?"

His demeanor subdued, he looked embarrassed.

"I loved the Corps and everything it stood for, but when I realized that the lives of 18- and 19-year old kids would be in my hands, I knew I wasn't ready to lead them. I may never be ready to lead them. I told my commander and he suggested I sleep on it a few days. Those few days only solidified my feelings."

Al's lips were pursed and his eyes glistened. I was shocked. For a few seconds, I didn't know what to say.

"You made the right decision. It took a hell of a lot more courage to do what you did than to stay against your better judgment. I am proud of you," and I hugged him.

"I don't know. I think about my buddies who are serving in the Middle East, and I feel guilty."

"Hey, you don't owe them anything, except maybe the truth. Don't let the Catholic guilt thing work on your head. Do you think they've been honest with themselves? How many of them would have had the guts to do what you did? You saved those kids' lives, and maybe your own life by listening to your conscience and making a difficult decision. I admire you, Al."

As he drove away, I thought about all the questions I had had while lying in the hospital bed at Camp Zama, before opting to go home. Why did I turn my back on my teammates, my brothers? Was I a coward for choosing life and the relative safety of a stateside assignment? What did my teammates think of me?

I had mixed emotions that evening in the parking lot as Al drove off, because I knew his decision would haunt him every day for the rest of his life.

Veterans' Writing Groups

I wasn't sure what to expect when I first joined the Syracuse Veterans' Writing Group, except perhaps that I'd meet other veterans like me with lots of questions, but few answers. I've met terrific men and women veterans, many of them my sons' ages, who ask the same questions I did: *What did I accomplish in the war zone? Do I have any regrets, either in what I did, or in what I didn't do? What did I learn about myself? What should I do with the rest of my life?* Some of our members didn't know that they had questions until we shared each other's work. We pursue these questions as writers in hopes of finding answers, but I've come to realize that I may never have all the answers I want.

As I wrote and shared my stories in the writing group, I noticed that they had a positive impact on younger vets. I could see their expressions, a visceral reaction as I read chapter after chapter of this memoir. I speak their language and feel their pain. Despite different ages and different wars, we share a common experience. As I wrote, I realized that my stories were not about Vietnam or about me, but about all combatants, all wars.

There is no glory in war. There is no honor in war. There is no God in war. I was angry at the government for lying to me. I still am. They knew exactly how to get my attention. I was ready to prove that I was a man, but at 21 years of age, I didn't have a clue what being a man meant. I hated myself for believing what the recruiter said about valor and heroism. Becoming a Green Beret didn't make me a man. Caring about other human beings did, but it took me almost 50 years to learn that lesson.

I will never forget what I saw and did in a war zone. It has colored my life, yet my experience may not be the same as another vet. Time, place, and circumstance notwithstanding, the military has changed very little since the Vietnam Conflict. War is trauma and we vets have that in common.

When I started this writer's journey, there was little to be proud of—I didn't like me, couldn't look myself in the mirror. I've struggled for over twelve years to find out who that man is hiding under the Green Beret, and the image is coming into focus. I think I can love him now, because he's a good person, a fallible human being despite what Special Forces taught him.

There are many things about the military that have served me well. I believe in a purpose-driven life. I'm results oriented and loyal to a fault, as long as there is trust. But I'm not a stone-cold killer, and will never again ignore my moral compass. I have to live with myself for the years I have left.

Jonathan Shay, the VA psychiatrist responsible for the development of the VA's Behavioral Health Program, has said that he learned all he knows about posttraumatic stress disorder and moral injury from veterans. That's because veterans heal veterans. I'm encouraged by the reactions of these young veterans to my writing. They've embraced me in a way I could not have imagined.

Frankly, you don't need to be a veteran to be traumatized. Humans share a common experience. I began speaking about my trauma to civilian groups and realized that my experience transcends boundaries. People talk to me about their own trauma: losing a child, being beaten or raped, or seriously injured in an accident. Sharing my burden with other people reminds me about the commonality of the human experience.

I spent a lifetime lamenting that I hadn't become a healer, a saver of lives. Now I wonder if I ever would have felt this fulfilled had I become a doctor.

MILITARY TERMS DEFINED

AC-47	Specially fitted gunship; "Spooky"
AIT	Advanced Infantry Training
APC	Armored Personnel Carrier
ARVN	Army of the Republic of Vietnam
A-Team	Special Forces 12-man operational detachment
B-Team	Special Forces support detachment
C-7 Caribou	Tactical aircraft carrying up to 21 troops
CH-47 Chinook	Helicopter carrying up to 35 troops; "Shithook"
Charlie	Viet Cong; Victor Charlie
CIB	Combat Infantryman Badge
CIDG	Civilian Irregular Defense Group
Class A Uniform	Dress uniform
CO	Commanding Officer
C-Team	Special Forces headquarters
DZ	Drop Zone
ETS	Estimated Time of Separation
FAO	Forward Air Observer
Fatigues	Military workwear uniform
FNG	Fucking New Guy
Frag	Kill someone with a grenade
FTX	Field Training Exercise
H&I	Harass and Interdict
KKK	Khmer Kampuchea Krom
Klick	Kilometer

MILITARY TERMS DEFINED

Leg	Nonairborne soldier
Lifer	Carrier soldier
LRRP	Long-range reconnaissance patrol rations
LZ	Landing Zone
McGuire Rig	Extraction device made of nylon straps
NCO	Noncommissioned Officer
Nûngs	Chinese ethnic group in Vietnam
NVA	North Vietnamese Army
Ops	Operations
PRC-25	Radio
SF	Special Forces
SFA	Special Forces Association
SFG	Special Forces Group
SOG	Studies and Observations Group (Special Operations)
Spec 4	Specialist 4
Strikers	Cambodian and Nûng mercenaries
Tactical Zone	One of four geographic areas in South Vietnam
Top	Team master sergeant; most senior NCO
Training Group	Special Forces Training Group
TZ	Tactical Zone
UH1-D	"Huey" helicopter
Viet Cong	Enemy guerrillas; Victor Charlie
Yard	Montagnard (Indigenous tribesman)
XO	Executive Officer

About the Author

Peter (Pete) McShane served as a US Army Special Forces medic during the Vietnam conflict, 1967–1968. A graduate of Syracuse University with an MBA, he had a career in banking and finance, much of it as a consultant to small businesses, saving them from their creditors and themselves. Now he writes. Pete has completed a collection of short stories, a novella, a number of personal essays, and recently finished a memoir, with another on the way. His other interests include hiking, cycling, and listening to rhythm and blues.

Thanks for reading! Please add a short review wherever you purchased the book, or on Goodreads. Check out my website (http:\\www.petermcshane.com) for appearances and reading dates, find other stories and a gallery of photos and memorabilia from my tour in Vietnam.

Acknowledgments

I would like to thank the magazines and journals that previously published some of the stories in this book. I am grateful for the support of the YMCA's Downtown Writers Center, Phil Memmer, Georgia Popoff, and the talented instructors and classmates who workshopped many of these stories. I would like to thank Eileen Schell, Ivy Kleinbart, and the members of the Syracuse Veterans' Writing Group for encouragement and support. To Denis Chericone who walked me through my darkest days after the reunion and was there as these stories took shape, I say thank you, my friend. To Marcia Trahan, Margaret Diehl, and Steve Parks who provided editorial guidance, thank you. I am grateful for the VA Behavioral Health community, the psychiatrists, psychologists, and clinical social workers who have made such a difference in my life, and finally to Linda, my loving wife, who was with me at the reunion and has traveled this journey with me, day by day, word for word—I couldn't have done this without you. My love always.

Made in the USA
Middletown, DE
08 June 2018